ENGLISH
in Common

5

Workbook

Mark Foley

Series Consultants
María Victoria Saumell and Sarah Louisa Birchley

ALWAYS LEARNING

PEARSON

English in Common 5
Workbook

Pearson Education, 10 Bank Street, White Plains, NY 10606

Staff credits: The editorial, design, production, and
manufacturing people who make up the *English in Common 5*
team are Margaret Antonini, Allen Ascher, Rhea Banker, Eleanor
Kirby Barnes, Peter Benson, Mike Boyle, Tracey Cataldo, Aerin
Csigay, Dave Dickey, Chris Edmonds, Mike Kemper, Laurie
Neaman, Daria Ruzicka, Loretta Steeves, Katherine Sullivan, Jeff
Zeter, and Charlie Green.

This series is dedicated to Charlie Green. Without Charlie's
knowledge of pedagogy, strong work ethic, sense of humor,
patience, perseverance, and creativity, *English in Common* would
never have existed.

Cover design: Tracey Cataldo
Cover photo: © qushe/shutterstock.com
Text design: Tracey Cataldo
Text composition: TSI Graphics
Text font: MetaPlus

ISBN 13: 978-0-13-262902-7
ISBN 10: 0-13-262902-X

Library of Congress Cataloging-in-Publication Data
Bygrave, Jonathan
    English in common. Book 1 / Jonathan Bygrave.
        p. cm.
ISBN 0-13-247003-9—ISBN 0-13-262725-6—
ISBN 0-13-262727-2—ISBN 0-13-262728-0—
ISBN 0-13-262729-9—ISBN 0-13-262731-0
1. English language—Textbooks for foreign speakers.
2. English language—Grammar.
3. English language—Spoken English.
    PE1128.B865 2011
    428.24—dc23

2011024736

Printed in the United States of America
6   16

Photo Credits: All photos are used under license from
Shutterstock.com except for the following. Page 4 Photos 12/
Alamy; p. 14 DBURKE/Alamy; p. 22 Blend Images/Alamy;
p. 28 Robert Edwards Drawn & Quartered/Newscom; p. 33
(top) Digital Vision/Punchstock, (bottom) Dreamstime.com;
p. 44 Comstock/Punchstock; p. 46 Dreamstime.com; p. 54
Daily Mail/Rex/Alamy; p. 56 Digital Vision/Punchstock.

Illustration Credits: John Batten, David Shenton, Roger Wade-
Walker

Contents

A **Workbook Answer Key** is provided on *ActiveTeach* at the back of the Teacher's Resource Book. Click on the Printable Resources tab at the bottom of the screen.

Reading

1a Read the article about *Friends*. Match descriptions with paragraphs 1–5.

_____ **a.** Explains the background of *Friends*.

_____ **b.** Describes some negative reactions to the show.

_____ **c.** Introduces us to the theme.

_____ **d.** Gives factual information about the *Friends* series.

_____ **e.** Explains the success of the show in an international context.

b Read the article again. Answer the questions on a separate sheet of paper.

1. Were any of the main actors in *Friends* famous before the show began?
2. Was the show popular in the early days?
3. Who invented the show?
4. Why do people like the characters in *Friends*?
5. What creates most of the comedy in the show?
6. Which two features made it hard to believe in the characters?
7. How did the producers try to keep the show interesting?
8. What was missing by the end of the series?

c Find words and phrases in the article that mean:

1. make a lot of money (*adj.*) (paragraph 2) _____
2. was suggested formally or put forward (*v.*) (paragraph 2) _____
3. equal to or the same as (*n.*) (paragraph 2) _____
4. statistics that show how many people watch something (*n.*) (paragraph 3) _____
5. watched a particular TV station (*phr. v.*) (paragraph 3) _____
6. attractive and appealing (*adj.*) (paragraph 4) _____
7. something that unifies people (*n.*) (paragraph 4) _____
8. lost its energy (*phrase*) (paragraph 5) _____

The F·R·I·E·N·D·S Phenomenon

① Everybody loves their friends. But do you love *Friends*? If you are one of the half a billion people that have seen this hugely popular American TV show, then the answer is probably "yes."

② By far the most successful and profitable comedy series of recent times, *Friends* has been shown in more than 30 countries around the world. The series was nominated for a record number of 44 Emmys, which is American TV's equivalent of the Oscars. The previously-unknown actors who played the main characters are now international household names and multi-millionaires.

③ It was first shown in the USA in 1994. The show quickly became a favorite, achieving top ratings. When the final episode was shown in 2004, more than 52 million people tuned in to watch. The show became so popular that by the time of the ninth season each of its six stars was able to command a fee of $1.5 million *per episode*!

④ Created by writers Marta Kauffman and David Crane, the series followed the romantic and personal adventures of a group of six friends in their 20s and early 30s living in New York City. Kauffman and Crane were careful to create a cast of believable characters that almost everybody could identify with. Like real people, each character had both endearing and irritating qualities. They were very different from each other, but shared a common bond in their friendship and loyalty. It was the interaction between these contrasting personalities that provided most of the humor in the show.

⑤ Although popular with the public, *Friends* was not always a hit with the critics. Some found it hard to believe in these young people who, although supposedly doing very ordinary jobs, seemed to lead lives of endless leisure in huge apartments. And over the years the producers began to become more and more dependent on bringing in new characters and guest stars in order to keep the show fresh. As a result, new or ex-boyfriends and girlfriends were always appearing. The focus on the six main characters, the magic ingredient in the show's early success, began to be lost. Most critics agreed that by the tenth season the show had run out of steam, and the announcement that episode number 238 would be the last came as no great surprise.

Writing

2a Read messages 1–3. Match with the writers a–c.

_____ **a.** a co-worker

_____ **b.** a friend

_____ **c.** a neighbor

①
> Bill,
> Thanks for agreeing to feed the cats!
> The cat food is on the top shelf in
> the cupboard.
> And don't forget to give them some
> water.
> I'm back on Thursday.
> Jerry

②
> **Party tonight at 9 P.M.**
> The ground floor apartment at
>   82 Mandeville Road.
> It is just behind a big Supersaver
>   supermarket.
> Bring some nice food!
> Francesca   X X

③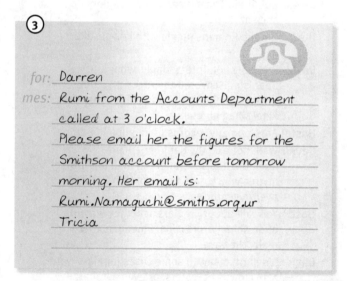
> *for:* Darren
> *mes:* Rumi from the Accounts Department
>   called at 3 o'clock.
>   Please email her the figures for the
>   Smithson account before tomorrow
>   morning. Her email is:
>   Rumi.Namaguchi@smiths.org.ur
>   Tricia

b In notes and messages unnecessary words are often left out. Underline at least five words in each message that can be left out.

Grammar

3 Complete the sentences with the correct tag questions.

1. We should have waited longer, _____?

2. Mr. Bolton couldn't come, _____?

3. Hardly anybody writes letters now, _____?

4. You went to Mexico last summer, _____?

5. Nothing works on this computer, _____?

6. You won't forget to call me, _____?

7. Nobody answered the ad, _____?

8. Help yourself to a drink, _____?

9. I'm late again, _____?

10. Let's get pizza this evening, _____?

4 Five of the tag questions are incorrect. Correct the mistakes.

1. Nobody likes cabbage, does he?

2. Let's get a taxi this time, shall we?

3. You can't use a cell phone on the plane, can't you?

4. Somebody told you, didn't he?

5. Leave the keys under the mat, will you?

6. Hilary isn't married, isn't she?

7. Nothing's expensive in this shop, are they?

8. Take one of my business cards, will you?

Communication

1a Read the transcript of a radio interview and choose the best title. _____
  a. The Recent History of Juggling
  b. Different Types of Juggling around the World
  c. Juggling in Ancient Times

b Read the interview again and mark the statements true (*T*) or false (*F*).
  _____ 1. David Sanchez is a juggler.
  _____ 2. Professional jugglers use the term "toss juggling."
  _____ 3. The earliest picture of jugglers is from ancient China.
  _____ 4. There is a picture of Egyptian jugglers in a museum in Berlin.
  _____ 5. There is no evidence of juggling in the Americas.
  _____ 6. There were probably jugglers in Ireland in ancient times.
  _____ 7. Some jugglers were also clowns or jesters.

c Now read the interview and find words that mean:
  1. writer of a particular book _____
  2. throwing _____
  3. a place where someone is buried _____
  4. metal weapons with sharp blades _____
  5. restricted to one area _____
  6. stories invented about the past _____
  7. connected _____

Host: On today's *Meet the Author,* we're talking to David Sanchez, juggler and author of *A Short History of Juggling.* David, welcome to the show.

David: Thanks.

Host: Now, I suppose we all have a broad idea of what juggling is, but could you tell us what **you** mean by "juggling"?

David: Sure. I pretty much stick to the traditional idea of juggling. I think the dictionary calls it "keeping two or more objects in the air at one time by alternately tossing and catching them." In the profession we call that "toss juggling." I think that's the type of juggling most people are familiar with.

Host: Has juggling been around for a long time?

David: Oh, yes. I found references to juggling from more than 3,000 years ago. There are some Egyptian tomb paintings that show jugglers from the Middle Kingdom period, and there's an ancient Egyptian statue of a juggler in the Staatliche museum in Berlin.

Host: What about written records?

David: Well, the earliest written record we know of is from ancient China. There's a book from the 3rd or 4th century B.C. that describes a juggler who could throw seven swords in the air.

Host: That sounds like something from one of those Chinese martial-arts movies!

David: Yes, juggling with swords is a well-established tradition in East Asia.

Host: So, was juggling confined to the Middle East and Asia in ancient times?

David: Not at all. There were lots of jugglers in ancient Rome.

Host: Did the Romans juggle with knives, like the Chinese?

David: Probably not. Interestingly, when the Spanish discovered the Americas, they noted in their reports and diaries that the Aztecs had jugglers.

Host: Are there any records of juggling in Europe?

David: Well, not exactly, but jugglers are mentioned in several of the Irish and Norse myths, which date from the fifth to the twelfth centuries.

Host: You talk about jugglers as if they were part of an actual profession. I mean, is that really the case?

David: It's hard to say. In some cases jugglers were also clowns or jesters, or even acrobats.

Host: Yes, I can see how the skills might be linked. Now, can you tell us about the more recent history of juggling . . .

Grammar

2 Complete the article using words from the box.

> everybody anybody only all
> everything nothing some
> somebody something anything

Goodbye to CDs

In the old days, the _____ (1.) way to get your favorite pop song was to walk into a music store and buy a CD. But _____ (2.) stays the same in the world of technology. When you talk to people today, they are _____ (3.) getting their music from the Internet. The result is that many music stores are experiencing dropping sales, and can often be virtually deserted.

Nowadays, it seems _____ (4.) is downloading songs as digital files from the Internet and listening to them on MP3 players and cell phones. _____ (5.) who still buys their music from a store is regarded as a dinosaur!

In fact, in the US, the list of the most popular songs is now based equally on sales in music stores and on the number of songs downloaded from the Internet. Recording companies have recognized the importance of this new way of distributing music and _____ (6.) you could possibly want to hear is now available in digital form. From the latest avant-garde groups, to the most obscure medieval church music, there is always _____ (7.) ready and willing to record even the most unusual piece of music and upload it onto the Internet.

Of course, _____ (8.) that can be downloaded to one computer can also be downloaded to another illegally, and it's free to trade music tracks with your friends. But _____ (9.) musicians aren't happy about this because it deprives them of royalties. They believe _____ (10.) should be done to prevent what they feel is basically theft.

3 Rewrite the sentences using words from the box in Exercise 2 to replace the underlined phrases. Make changes as needed.

Ex: There are <u>no good shows</u> to watch on TV.
   There is nothing to watch on TV.

1. <u>None of the contestants</u> won any prizes.
   _____

2. Would you like <u>a glass</u> of water?
   _____

3. We've been through <u>all the files</u> and we can't find your application form.
   _____

4. I'm sorry, but we don't have <u>any hotel rooms</u> available in July.
   _____

5. <u>All the people</u> on my street own cars.
   _____

6. I waited at the front desk for a long time but I couldn't find <u>a single person</u> to help me.
   _____

7. We've got lots of silk dresses, but I'm afraid we have <u>no silk dresses</u> in your size.
   _____

8. Mei Ling ate <u>every piece</u> of her birthday cake.
   _____

Vocabulary

4 Complete the missing word in each sentence.

1. My nephew's very a_____c. He loves painting.
2. I am r_____e for our after-sales service.
3. Ice-skating well requires great s_____l.
4. Never underestimate the i_____e of having good friends.
5. Dorotea runs a very s_____l business.
6. People in big cities are often more l_____y than people in small towns.

5 Match the beginning of each sentence with its end.

____ 1. I couldn't	a. true.
____ 2. I totally	b. completely true.
____ 3. I'm not sure if	c. agree more.
____ 4. That's probably	d. in that.
____ 5. I don't think that's	e. disagree.
____ 6. I think there's some truth	f. I agree with that.

Communication

1a Read the conversations. Match each one with its situation.

____ **a.** on a train   ____ **c.** a survey

____ **b.** in a store   ____ **d.** in a cafe

Conversation 1

W: Excuse me. We're doing a survey on cell phones. Could I ask you a few questions?

M: Sure.

W: Do you own a cell phone?

M: Yes.

W: And what do you mainly use it for?

M: Sending text messages, I guess.

W: How many would you send on an average day?

M: Well, about five or six usually.

W: And are those mainly for business or social purposes?

M: Social. I can't use my phone at work—I'm a pilot.

Conversation 2

M: Honestly. You want some peace and quiet and all you hear are those awful cell phones non-stop. It drives me crazy!

W: Yeah, and people talk about a lot of nonsense, don't they? "Um, I'm on the train, and now we're pulling into a station . . ."

M: Some of these people must have more money than sense. It must cost an arm and a leg to make all those calls.

W: Maybe they have a cheap calling plan.

Conversation 3

J: Is that a new cell phone Steve?

S: Yeah. I got it on sale.

J: It looks very sophisticated.

S: Mmm. It has a camera and an MP3 player.

J: So you can listen to all the latest tracks . . .

S: Exactly. But the really cool thing is that it sends text messages with the latest soccer results. Get one, John. They had tons in stock.

Conversation 4

M: Which model are you interested in, miss?

W: I'm not sure. I want a phone that takes photos.

M: OK. Most of them do that now anyway.

W: Oh, I see. Well, I like to keep in touch with the kids when I'm overseas, so I need a phone that works in other countries.

M: In that case, you need a "triband" phone then. Anything else?

W: Yes, I want something that's really small and light, you know, easy to carry around.

M: Well, what about this Minirola? We have a ten day trial period. If you're not happy with it, you could bring it back and we'll refund your money.

---

b Read the conversations again. Then correct the mistakes in the statements below.

Conversation 1

1. The man only uses his phone to send text messages.

2. He's able to use his phone at work.

Conversation 2

3. The man expects train journeys to be noisy.

4. The woman thinks it's expensive to make cell phone calls.

Conversation 3

5. Steve paid full price for his cell phone.

6. John doesn't like Steve's new phone.

Conversation 4

7. The customer doesn't have any children.

8. If she isn't happy after 10 days, the customer can get a different phone.

c Read the conversations again. Match these words and phrases with their meanings.

____ **1.** non-stop

____ **2.** drives me crazy

____ **3.** cost an arm and a leg

____ **4.** calling plan

____ **5.** on sale

____ **6.** tracks

____ **7.** the really cool thing

____ **8.** tons

a. has a reduced price

b. songs or short pieces of music

c. a large quantity

d. all the time

e. prices for using a service

f. makes me very upset

g. be very expensive

h. something particularly impressive

Vocabulary

2   Complete the sentences with appropriate words.

1. Does your dog _____ at the vacuum cleaner? Mine does!
2. I _____ when I saw a spider in the bathtub.
3. The walls are so thin we can hear our neighbor's phone _____.
4. Our house is very old, so all the floors _____.
5. She was so angry she _____ her fist on the table.

Grammar

3   Look at the sentences. Match them with their purposes below.

Conversation 1

____ 1. *Could* I ask you a few questions?

____ 2. I *can't* use my phone at work

Conversation 2

____ 3. It *must* cost an arm and a leg

Conversation 3

____ 4. It has a camera, and it *can* play MP3 files.

Conversation 4

____ 5. You *could* bring it back.

a. describing an ability
b. asking for permission
c. describing a future possibility
d. saying that something isn't allowed
e. making a strong prediction

4   Read the article. Circle the correct choices to complete it.

The Miracle Chip

British scientists at the Imperial College in London today announced plans to begin trials of a new device that *must/could/can't* (**1.**) revolutionize the lives of people with serious medical conditions. The device is a tiny sensor that *can/might/may* (**2.**) monitor changes in the body and is able to send out warning signals via a cell phone.

The sensor, a microchip, is put under the patient's skin and *can't/can/might* (**3.**) detect any dangerous changes long before the patient is even aware of them. This means that patients with serious conditions who would usually have to stay in the hospital *can/must/can't* (**4.**) now live at home and *could/must/can't* (**5.**) lead more normal lives.

When it detects changes in the body, the microchip sends out a pre-programmed text message to the patient's doctor or hospital, describing the changes in detail. Of course, patients with the device *may/could/have to* (**6.**) carry their cell phone with them at all times, but this will be the only restriction on their lifestyles.

Although it will probably be expensive to develop, the device *can't/could/must* (**7.**) be a boon to the economy because those patients who *can't/could/can* (**8.**) work because of the need to be near medical facilities will be able to go back to full-time employment. This could save the government millions in sickness and unemployment benefits.

The first patients to be given the implant will be diabetics, but doctors hope to extend the trial to those with heart or lung diseases. And, it's possible that in years to come the device *might/can/can't* (**9.**) be adapted to cover even more conditions.

If all goes according to the plan and the trial is a success, the device *can/couldn't/could* (**10.**) be available to the general public within three to four years.

1 Complete the crossword.

Across

1. He's the son of my mother's new husband. He's my ____-brother.
3. They'd been married for ten years before his ____ got sick.
7. I don't see eye to ____ with my sister.
8. He made a good ____ on his new boss.
9. I have two ____-sisters from my mother's previous marriage.
10. Brianne's a ____ of mine—we both work at the travel agency.

Down

2. She isn't married, but she has a ____.
3. I'm on the same ____ as she is; we feel the same way about things.
4. I don't know him very well. He's only an ____.
5. He's an old friend; we are very ____.
6. She's perfect for you. I'm sure you'll ____ with her.

2 Circle the correct choice.

1. Somebody has been using my toothbrush, *haven't they/hasn't he*?
2. I'm going to be late, *aren't/are* I?
3. We pay here, *don't/can't* we?
4. They could have called, *could have/couldn't* they?
5. Miranda never eats meat, *doesn't/does* she?
6. *Something/Nothing* needs to be done, doesn't it?
7. We hardly ever go to the movies, *don't/do* we?
8. Have a piece of cake, *haven't/won't* you?

3 Check (✓) the sentences that are correct and put an ✗ by the sentences that are incorrect. Both sentences in a pair can be correct or incorrect.

1. ____ a. I wasn't able to find anything that fit me.
   ____ b. I wasn't able to find nothing that fit me.

2. ____ a. Would you like any dessert?
   ____ b. Would you like some dessert?

3. ____ a. There's anything wrong with this phone.
   ____ b. There's something wrong with this phone.

4. ____ a. Everything on the list were unavailable.
   ____ b. Anything on the list were unavailable.

5. ____ a. Did anyone call while I was out?
   ____ b. Did someone call while I was out?

6. ____ a. I've tried anything. It still doesn't work.
   ____ b. I've tried everything. It still doesn't work.

7. ____ a. There's nowhere to store things in my apartment.
   ____ b. There are nowhere to store things in my apartment.

8. ____ a. We're bored; we don't have everything to do.
   ____ b. We're bored; we don't have anything to do.

4 Complete the description using words from the box. Some words are not used.

importance	important	artistic	skill
loneliness	lonely	jealous	
responsible	successful	success	

I come from quite a large family. The great thing about a large family is that you never feel _____ (1.) because there's always someone to talk to.

My older brother, James, is a university professor. He's very smart; his hobby is reading Greek philosophy! I'm the _____ (2.) one in the family. I'm a graphic designer. My twin brother, Seth, is the practical one. He's a carpenter and he can do amazing things with wood. It's a _____ (3.) I really admire.

But my younger sister, Kate, is the most _____ (4.) of us all; she's the managing director of a huge company. She is _____ (5.) for more than 250 workers. Of course, she has a big salary, which we are all a little _____ (6.) of! But in the end, money doesn't matter. The _____ (7.) thing is that we all support each other.

5 Complete the sentences with words from the box. Change the forms as necessary. Some words are not used.

crash	bark	snore	ring
creak	scream	thud	bang

1. Bob's _____ kept me awake all night!
2. Katrina _____ when she saw the accident.
3. I hate dogs that _____ all the time.
4. Put some oil on that door; it _____ whenever you open it.
5. Please don't _____ the door when you leave!
6. My cell phone doesn't _____, it vibrates.

6 Circle the correct words below to complete the conversation.

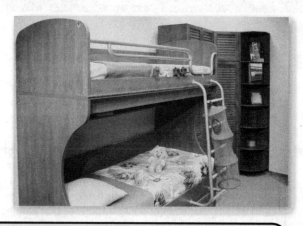

Jim: Where are the kids? They're not in the bedroom.
Sue: I'm not sure. They ____ (1.) be playing in the garage.
Jim: No, they ____ (2.) be there—it's locked.
Sue: Oh, they ____ (3.) be in the backyard then. There's nowhere else.
Jim: OK. I'll have a look. (*Two minutes later*) Well, they aren't there.
Sue: I guess they ____ (4.) be next door, although it's unlikely.
Jim: No, they ____ (5.) be there. The neighbors are on vacation.
Sue: You're right. What about the park? They ____ (6.) be there.
Jim: But the park is closed on Sunday afternoons.
Sue: That's not true. You ____ (7.) go there until six o'clock.
Jim: Well, perhaps we should go and get them.
Sue: Yes, we'll take your car.
Jim: No, we ____ (8.). I loaned it to my sister.
Sue: Oh, yes. I forgot. Well, let's ask John, he ____ (9.) let us use his car.

1.	a. can	b. might	c. must
2.	a. can't	b. must	c. might
3.	a. could	b. must	c. can't
4.	a. can't	b. must	c. could
5.	a. must	b. can't	c. might
6.	a. can	b. might	c. couldn't
7.	a. must	b. might	c. can
8.	a. can't	b. might	c. must
9.	a. couldn't	b. must	c. might

Making a living

Communication

1a Read four people's descriptions of their jobs.

Speaker 1

I'm a natural show off, I suppose. Even as a kid, I loved performing in front of other people. Whenever the family got together, my parents used to get me to stand on the table, singing songs and doing little scenes. There's a sort of buzz that you get from an audience that nothing else quite matches up to. In fact, I _____ on stage again next month, which should make a nice change from all the TV work.

Speaker 2

It all happened by accident, really. I mean—I never meant to get into this line of work. In fact, when I was young, I wanted to be a ballerina! But when I was in college, a friend persuaded me to take some pictures for the college magazine, and it all sort of snowballed from there. The fashion shoots are the ones I enjoy most. But I'm freelance, so basically I _____ any assignment that's offered. Even weddings!

Speaker 3

The really great thing about my job is the number and variety of people you meet. Not that they are all nice— some of the guests are a real handful! But however bad they are, you always know that they _____ in a few days, so that makes it bearable. And of course, I often get the chance to practice my foreign language.

Speaker 4

Even when I was really small, I loved drawing. I had a thing for space ships and futuristic cities for some reason! Well, of course, I don't really do any actual drawing now—the computers do it all for us! But designing is something that's in the blood, and the great thing about my job is that it's not just theoretical, because you know real people _____ and work in the things you've designed . . .

b Match each speaker with a job from the box. Some jobs are not used.

ballet dancer	engineer	secretary
photographer	architect	actor
hotel receptionist	journalist	

Speaker 1 _____   Speaker 3 _____

Speaker 2 _____   Speaker 4 _____

c Complete these expressions used by the Speakers. Then match the expressions with the definitions below.

Speaker 1

1. I'm a natural _____, I suppose.
2. There's a sort of _____ that you get from an audience . . .

Speaker 2

3. . . . I never meant to get into this _____.
4. . . . it all sort of _____ from there.
5. But I'm _____, so basically . . .

Speaker 3

6. . . . some of the guests are _____!

Speaker 4

7. I had _____ space ships and futuristic cities for some reason!
8. . . . designing is something that's _____.

_____ **a.** difficult to manage *or* deal with
_____ **b.** person who likes to be the center of attention
_____ **c.** an obsession with
_____ **d.** developed *or* grew rapidly
_____ **e.** career or profession
_____ **f.** part of your basic personality
_____ **g.** feeling of excitement
_____ **h.** self-employed

d Complete the descriptions in Exercise 1a using future forms of the verbs in the box.

| appear | take | leave | live |

Vocabulary

2 Complete the sentences using the correct forms of the expressions from the box. Some expressions are not used.

> have an eye for detail   be a self-starter
> be a people person   be a good listener
> do volunteer work   be promoted
> be good with numbers   be a team player
> have a "can do" attitude   retire early
> stay calm under pressure
> be able to meet tight deadlines
> bring out the best in other people

Ex: Thuy's really good at seeing all the small things in documents and reports.
Thuy *has an eye for detail.*

1. It doesn't matter how rushed he is, Javier always gets things finished on time.
Javier _____.

2. Working with Selena is great. She always seems to encourage her colleagues to do well.
Selena _____.

3. Even when things are really hectic, Dimitri is able to stay relaxed.
Dimitri _____.

4. Seiko is at her best when she is huddled over her calculator working on numbers.
Seiko _____.

5. My mother helps at the local nursing home, although she doesn't get paid.
My mother _____.

6. Alison is so positive, she thinks anything is possible.
Alison _____.

7. Jorge really excels when he is working as part of a group.
Jorge _____.

8. Yeon-oo wanted to travel, so she quit work when she was only 55.
Yeon-oo _____.

9. Rachel doesn't need any guidance. She always manages to think of what to do on her own.
Rachel _____.

10. After working as a salesman for ten years, Fernando is sales manager at last.
Fernando _____.

Grammar

3 Complete the sentences using the correct forms of the words in parentheses.

1. I'm not really sure, but I think I _____ the Caesar salad. (try)

2. We're so excited about our vacation—we _____ the Great Wall of China! (see)

3. The meeting _____ at ten tomorrow so please be here by nine-thirty. (start)

4. No thanks, I'm full. I _____ any more. (think/not/have)

5. Peter hates buses so he _____ by car. (probably/come)

6. The company _____ the new factory on January 1 next year. (open)

7. Look at those dark clouds, I think there _____ a storm. (be)

8. Mia's very well qualified so she _____ to get the job. (be/bound)

9. I can't see you next Tuesday because I _____ a conference. (attend)

10. We haven't set an exact date but the wedding _____ sometime in the spring. (definitely/be)

4 Use the cues to write about your future plans and predictions *or* ideas.
Ex: think/take/bath/this evening
I think I'll take a bath this evening.

1. have decided/start/exercising
_____

2. not sure about/buy/that jacket
_____

3. plan on/have/lazy morning/Sunday
_____

4. bound/get/marry/one day
_____

5. probably/not win/lottery
_____

6. like/have/vacation
_____

Reading

1a Read the article. Answer the questions on a separate piece of paper.

1. What does the word *guilt* in the title refer to?
2. Why is the weight of the sculpture significant?
3. What happens to 90% of electronic waste?

Sculpture of Guilt

① This is "Weee Man," a terrifying metal and plastic sculpture created by Paul Bonomini from discarded computers, electronic components, and domestic products. It was commissioned by the Royal Society of Arts (RSA). The sculpture is 24 feet (7 meters) tall, beside the Thames River in London, and serves as a shocking reminder of the huge amount of waste produced by today's extravagant high-tech society.

② The main body of the figure includes 12 washing machines, 10 refrigerators, 7 vacuum cleaners, 35 cell phones and 12 kettles, plus assorted microwaves, televisions, radiators and sections of pipes and cables. The artist has ingeniously created the head from some surprising elements. The teeth are computer mice, the eyes are washing machine doors and the ears are satellite dishes.

③ The name of the sculpture, "Weee," comes from Waste Electrical and Electronic Equipment. Its weight, 3.3 tons, is the same as the weight of electrical equipment thrown away by an average person in a lifetime. The RSA hopes that the sculpture will encourage recycling by dramatically reminding us of how many products we throw away unnecessarily. Citizens of the European Union currently produce 6.5 million tons of electronic waste a year, most of which ends up in landfill sites or is incinerated. Only 10% is recycled.

b Read the article again and find two more examples to add to each column in the chart.

Adjectives	Adverbs	Parts of the human body	Electronic equipment	Domestic appliances
terrifying	*ingeniously*	*head*	*computers*	*washing machines*

c Find words or phrases in the article that mean:

1. thrown away (*adj.*) (paragraph 1) _____
2. when somebody paid an artist to make a particular work (*v.*) (paragraph 1) _____
3. wasteful (*adj.*) (paragraph 1) _____
4. advanced technology (*compound adj.*) (paragraph 1) _____
5. wires connecting electrical appliances (*n.*) (paragraph 2) _____
6. devices held in your hand that control computers (*n.*) (paragraph 2) _____
7. promote *or* persuade (*v.*) (paragraph 3) _____
8. at the present time (*adv.*) (paragraph 3) _____
9. places where garbage is stored and then covered over with earth (*compound n.*) (paragraph 3) _____
10. burned (*v.*) (paragraph 3) _____

Grammar

2 Answer to the questions using the cues and the correct future form.

Ex: A: Will you have finished work by five-thirty tomorrow?

  B: No, I/not finish/until six

  No, I won't have finished until six.

1. **A:** Will you be going on vacation next July?

   B: No, I/go/in August, instead

   _____

   _____

2. **A:** Do you think Marco will have finished the project by the time I get back?

   B: Yes, he/should/finish/it by then

   _____

   _____

3. **A:** Will Mr. Simpson be able to see me between four and five?

   B: No, I'm afraid he/see/another client then

   _____

   _____

4. **A:** Can we start work on the construction site next January?

   B: Yes, we/should/receive/planning permission/by then

   _____

   _____

5. **A:** Will the children be joining you for the summer?

   B: Yes, they/stay/with us from July to September

   _____

   _____

6. **A:** Can we meet in the office tomorrow afternoon?

   B: No, I/work/at home/all day tomorrow

   _____

   _____

7. **A:** How are you doing with the decorating?

   B: Pretty well. By the end of next month, we should/finish/most of it

   _____

   _____

8. **A:** Will Gabriella's report be ready for the meeting this afternoon?

   B: Yes, she/do/it by lunchtime at the latest

   _____

   _____

3 Complete the conversations using the future perfect or future continuous forms of the verbs in parentheses.

1. **A:** Can I watch the cartoons now, Mom?

   B: No. You can wait until after dinner.

   A: But they _____ by then! (finish)

2. **A:** Do you think we'll get there in time?

   B: No, I don't. By the time we get there the train _____. (leave)

3. **A:** Next week's going to be really busy.

   B: Not for me! This time next week I _____ on a beach in Jamaica. (lie)

4. **A:** Is Suyin coming to the party on her own?

   B: No. She _____ her boyfriend. (bring)

5. **A:** I don't want to spend hours waiting for her at the airport.

   B: Don't worry. I'm sure Jan _____ by the time we get there. (arrive)

Vocabulary

4 Four sentences contain mistakes. Correct the mistakes.

1. On the weekends, I like to social with my friends.

2. A good way to meet new people is to make night classes.

3. It's important to spend quality time for your children.

4. My sister's going to study for a degree online.

5. You should always try to keep up to day with your emails.

6. By the end of the month, we'll have finished painting the apartment.

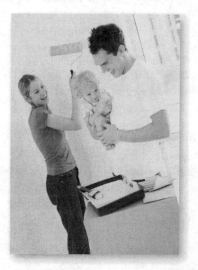

Reading

1a Read the newspaper excerpts. Mark the word *work* in the headlines as adjective (*adj.*), noun phrase (*n. phr.*), or phrasal verb (*phr. v.*).

A

Report claims night-shift work can damage health

A report published today claims that people who work the night shift suffer from significantly worse health than those working regular hours. Scientists in Frankfurt examined 400 factory workers, half of whom worked the night shift, and compared their health with regular office staff.

B

Car makers reduce work force by 10,000

A leading Japanese car maker has announced massive lay-offs at its Tokyo plant. Half of the 20,000 workers are likely to be laid off. A spokesman for Hon-Tang Automotive explained that disappointing sales of its new sedan were to blame for the decision.

C

"I work out twice a week," admits overweight TV star

Len Travis, star of television's hit series *Fight the Flab*, has admitted he exercises regularly at a gym in West London. Len, 45, was spotted by a press reporter while leaving the exclusive health club. The overweight actor had previously claimed that he never did any exercise and was "a total sloth."

D

Workaholic partners blamed for 40% of failed marriages

Sociologists at an American university have found that more than a third of divorces are caused by partners spending too little time at home. "Many husbands or wives spend as much as 50 hours a week away from home," claims senior researcher Carol Dimkins.

E

Government working on new cell phone regulations

The Department of Science and Technology is planning to introduce new laws governing the use of cell phones. A committee has been developing a series of new regulations designed to prevent the misuse of phones by children. Their proposals are likely to include the banning of all cell phones at schools and colleges.

F

"I'm still working class," claims millionaire rock star

Zed Taylor, lead singer with Canadian rock group The Zeds, has been defending his social background in a recent TV interview. Despite earning over $4 million last year and owning homes in Los Angeles and Vancouver, the singer, 32, says he is still the same as when he grew up in one of the poorest neighborhoods of Toronto.

b Read the excerpts again and answer the questions.

1. Which story discusses divorce? ____
2. Which story mentions employment problems in Tokyo? ____
3. Which story examines the lifestyle of a Canadian celebrity? ____
4. Which story cites a German study on the effect of working hours on the wellbeing of factory workers? ____

Grammar

2 Rewrite the sentences using *in case.*

Ex: We thought we might have to wait a long time so we took a lot of books.
We took a lot of books in case we had to wait a long time.

1. Maria took plenty of toys because she thought the children might get bored.
_____
_____

2. We're going to get extra copies of the keys made because we could lose one.
_____
_____

3. They may deliver the package this morning, so please listen for the doorbell.
_____
_____

4. Leave your cell phone turned on because I might need to contact you.
_____
_____

5. I thought the food on the train might be too expensive, so I took some sandwiches.
_____
_____

6. Eyeglasses often get broken, so you should take your spare pair.
_____
_____

7. We might see someone famous, so we're taking our camera with us.
_____
_____

8. There was a chance of rain, so they brought a couple of umbrellas.
_____
_____

Writing

3 Replace the underlined mistakes with words or phrases that are more appropriate for an application. Look at page 28 of the Student Book to help you.

> 79 Great North Way
> Minneapolis, MN 01443
> Tel: (555) 291-0423
>
> April 14, 2012
>
> Anna Sanchez
> Head of Human Resources
> Mega Travel Ltd
> PO Box 899
> Houston, TX 84215
>
> Dear *Head* (**1.**),
>
> I am writing to *make application for* (**2.**) the job of trainee travel agent *advertised by* (**3.**) this week's *Jobs Weekly*.
>
> *I think travel's really interesting* (**4.**) and I have visited several foreign countries in the last three or four years. I feel *I'd be very good for the job* (**5.**) because I have considerable personal experience of the problems travelers face in foreign countries. When I was in Mexico last year, I helped two Canadian tourists who had lost their travel tickets, and this *motivated me to feel very confident about myself* (**6.**).
>
> I recently completed my degree in Modern Languages at St. Paul University. I can speak *really good Spanish* (**7.**) and Italian, and I have a reasonable knowledge of French and Portuguese. *I have a fantastic knowledge* (**8.**) of the tourist resorts in Central America. I believe this would be a considerable advantage to a trainee travel agent in your company.
>
> I am 22 years old. I live in Minneapolis right now but I would *be OK about moving* (**9.**) to Houston if I was offered the job. *You can call me* (**10.**) on my cell phone number above at any time.
>
> Yours sincerely,
>
> *Danny Kingston*
>
> Danny Kingston

1 Complete the crossword.

Across

2. I work well with other people. I'm a ____ player.

5. You must be able to meet ____ deadlines. There's often only a few days to complete assignments.

7. The company my husband worked for was not doing well, so he was laid-____.

8. He's extremely precise. He has a real eye for ____.

10. He is always very positive. He has a can-do ____.

11. You should always stay calm under ____.

12. Dan's an accountant, so he's good with ____.

Down

1. He hated his job, so one day he just ____.

3. He knows how to bring out the ____ in people.

4. She loves company. She's a ____ person.

6. I can trust her to work on her own. She's a real self-____.

9. I can tell Ana all my problems. She's a good ____.

2 Circle the correct choice.

1. Miranda's been on *illness/sick* leave for the last three weeks.

2. He's only 50, but he's decided to *retire/quit* early from his job.

3. Peter *does/makes* a good living as an independent financial consultant.

4. Angela works *part-time/the night shift*, so she sometimes has to sleep during the day.

5. They closed down the factory and *fired/laid off* my uncle.

6. David *applied/quit* his job to care for his son.

3 Choose the best answer to complete each sentence.

____ 1. I won't be able to see you tomorrow because
   a. I go to the hair salon.
   b. I'm going to the hair salon.

____ 2. Look at the damage on these tires;
   a. they aren't going to last much longer.
   b. they aren't lasting much longer.

____ 3. I'm not very thirsty;
   a. I think I won't have anything to drink.
   b. I don't think I'll have anything to drink.

____ 4. David's such a good engineer—
   a. I think he'll get the job.
   b. I think he's getting the job.

____ 5. Tania's just given me the tickets—
   a. we're sitting in the front row.
   b. we're going to sit in the front row.

____ 6. That young pianist seems so talented;
   a. I believe he'll win the competition.
   b. I believe he's going to win the competition.

4 Complete the sentences using a future perfect or future continuous form of a verb from the box. Use *you* if necessary.

> finish   watch   repair   ask   relax   travel   clean   visit

1. Maria _____ all the rooms by the time the guests arrive.
2. By this time next week I _____ on a beach in the Caribbean.
3. _____ your brother play soccer on Saturday?
4. Do you think the technician _____ my computer by this afternoon?
5. By the end of the journey, she _____ more than 20,000 miles.
6. _____ preparing those numbers in time for the directors' meeting?
7. _____ your half-sister while you're in the States?
8. During the lunch break tomorrow, I _____ everybody to fill in a special questionnaire.

5 Match day-planner entries with descriptions. One of the descriptions is not needed.

Monday	1	meet Dave, Liz and Sue for dinner at restaurant 8 P.M.
Tuesday	2	Internet cafe—find hotels in Mazatlan
Wednesday	3	painting all day
Thursday	4	Internet cafe—unit 6 of accounting class
Friday	5	take Zoe and Bob to the zoo 9:30 – 12:00
Sat~~urday~~		~~ket~~

Descriptions

____ **a.** visit chat rooms   ____ **c.** do research on the Internet   ____ **e.** spend quality time with children

____ **b.** socialize with friends   ____ **d.** study for a qualification online   ____ **f.** redecorate the kitchen

6 Complete the sentences using *in case*.

1. I put on some insect repellent _____
_____ .

2. You'd better take an umbrella _____
_____ .

3. I always keep some aspirin _____
_____ .

4. I think you should put on some sunscreen
_____
_____ .

5. You should take a map _____
_____ .

7 Find and correct the eight mistakes in this blog.

I think one of the most important things in life is being happy at work. I'm a website designer, and I remember that when I applied to my current job, I told the interviewer I wasn't just crazy of design, I was passionate on it! Perhaps that's one of the reasons
5 I got the job. I suppose I'm really lucky because not only do I love my work, I also get along really well with my co-workers. They are all very different at me, but we all believe to what we are doing, so there's a great team spirit in the office. I work for a big advertising agency. It's a very busy and competitive business.
10 Some of my co-workers worry of that but I just get on and do my work. I think I'm pretty good of what I do and I'm really proud in some of the work I've done for the company.

Reading

1 Read the article about epic movies. Complete the article with the correct form of the verbs from the box.

> appear   be   have   make   come
> never appear   take   begin   earn

2a Read the article again. Complete the chart with a number or word.

Hollywood's greatest historical epics

Movie/Year	Notes
Gladiator, 2000	• earned more than $_____ (**1.**) at the box office
Ben Hur, _____ (**2.**)	• _____ (**3.**) by William Wyler
Spartacus, _____ (**4.**)	
El Cid, _____ (**5.**)	• the story of _____ (**6.**) hero
Lawrence of Arabia, 1962	• featuring a young Irish _____ (**7.**)
Cleopatra, _____ (**8.**)	• _____ (**9.**) Elizabeth Taylor
Troy, _____ (**10.**)	

b Read the article again. Which movie is the writer talking about?

1. perhaps the greatest epic of them all

   _____

2. Ridley Scott's inspiration for *Gladiator*

   _____

3. the most expensive movie ever made at the time _____

4. disappointing box office profits

   _____

5. went on to win five Oscars _____

One of the most remarkable developments in the recent history of movie-making _____ (**1.**) the revival of the historical epic. After being unpopular for almost 40 years, this genre of movie _____ (**2.**) an unexpected reappearance with Ridley Scott's *Gladiator*, in 2000. When it went on to win five Oscars, and to earn over $458 million at the box office, Hollywood was forced to re-examine this kind of movie.

So, what is a historical epic? To explain that, we have to go back to the late 1950s, and the movie *Ben Hur. Ben Hur*, which was directed by William Wyler, _____ (**3.**) all the ingredients of the historical epic: It was long, set in distant history, featured lots of battles, and it had big stars, and even bigger sets. The movie was released in 1959, and _____ (**4.**) six years to make and cost $15 million—the most expensive movie ever made at the time. But it went on to win Oscars and huge profits for MGM studios.

A series of superb epic movies followed. In 1960, director Stanley Kubrick made *Spartacus*, starring Kirk Douglas and Lawrence Olivier. The movie was Ridley Scott's inspiration for *Gladiator*. The next year, Charlton Heston, the star of *Ben Hur*, _____ (**5.**) with Sophia Loren in *El Cid*, the story of a Spanish hero. 1962 saw the release of perhaps the greatest epic of them all, David Lean's *Lawrence of Arabia*, featuring a young Irish actor who _____ (**6.**) on screen before, Peter O'Toole.

The end of this short golden age _____ (**7.**) in 1963, with the release of *Cleopatra*. The movie starred Elizabeth Taylor, cost a fortune to make, but was never able to make a profit at the box office. By the early 1960s, television _____ (**8.**) to outdo movies, theater attendance fell, and the amount of money movie makers _____ (**9.**) was simply too small to cover the enormous production costs of historical epics.

This changed in the late 1990s with computer generated imaging, or CGI as it is known. Suddenly, it was possible to have as many soldiers and horses, Roman arenas, and Trojan city walls as you wanted, without having to pay extras or build huge sets. But with the disappointing box office profits for *Troy*, in 2004 and *Alexander*, in 2005, perhaps this second golden age of the historical epic may be less than golden.

Grammar

3 Complete the sentences using the correct form of the verbs from the box.

> go   eat   meet   release
> lie   rain   work

1. David _____ an apple when he broke a tooth.
2. We were very excited because we _____ to Disneyland before.
3. By lunchtime, she was exhausted because she _____ hard all morning.
4. The weather was terrible. It _____ on the day we arrived and on the day we left!
5. When I opened the fridge, I found that my roommate _____ all the food!
6. Oliver Stone's film, *Alexander*, _____ in 2005.
7. When she came into the house, Carla's skin was very red—she _____ in the sun all day.
8. My mother _____ my father at a nightclub in 1982.

Vocabulary

4 Complete the sentences using words or phrases from the box. One is not used.

> for the previous   after that   since
> from that point on   at that time   during
> up until that point   while   until

1. _____ century, the two countries had been at war.
2. I stopped smoking three years ago, and I haven't had a single cigarette _____.
3. He got sick last year, but _____ he had been very healthy.
4. Mr. Reagan was President of the US _____ the 1980s.
5. It was the late 1950s, and _____ there were almost no supermarkets in the US.
6. We missed our connecting flight and _____ things just got worse.
7. Roberto used to take care of the children _____ Clara was at work.
8. The mechanic arrived and repaired our car. _____ we were able to continue on our trip.

Writing

5 These pictures tell a story. Write the story on a separate sheet of paper. Use the cues for each picture to help you.

Deborah/love/Tiddles
upset/when /missing
signs/offer/reward

Mr. and Mrs. Lopez/
enjoy/watch TV
TV/very old

one evening/something
wrong/picture
nothing wrong/TV set

take flashlight/outside
something wrong/
antenna?

see/cat
phone/fire station

firefighter/ladder/rescue

return/cat/Deborah
give/reward

use/money
buy/brand-new television

Vocabulary

1 Complete the crossword.

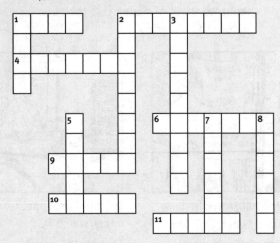

Across

1. the opposite of hard (*adj.*)
2. likely to make someone fall as a result of being wet (*adj.*)
4. material from an animal used for shoes and belts (*n.*)
6. many cheap toys are made of this hard material (*n.*)
9. like what an animal has on its skin (*adj.*)
10. having a bright surface (*adj.*)
11. makes you want to scratch your skin (*adj.*)

Down

1. a material that is often used in expensive clothing (*n.*)
2. slightly elastic (*adj.*)
3. antique vases are made from it (*n.*)
5. the opposite of smooth (*adj.*)
7. having an even surface (*adj.*)
8. a lightweight material that is good for summer clothes (*n.*)

Reading

2a Read the article. Answer the questions on a separate piece of paper.

1. What are *convenience stores*?
2. What is sometimes surprising about these places?
3. How do these stores find employees?
4. How are family members paid for their work?

Late-Night Shopping

Visitors to London, New York and Los Angeles often remark on how easy it is to buy _____ (**1.**) things at any time of the day or night. It isn't the well-known department stores, large supermarkets or huge shopping malls that they are talking about, but those tiny stores _____ (**2.**) Americans call "convenience stores" and the British call "corner shops."

They may not always be located on corners, but they are certainly convenient for tourists and for city-dwellers who work long hours and don't have time to shop during the day. As people in large cities work longer and longer hours, the availability of late-night shopping has become a necessity, rather than a luxury.

_____ (**3.**) other thing that sometimes causes surprise is that these shops are rarely owned or staffed by local people. The English-sounding names of "Super Saver," "Bargain Supplies," or "Mini-market" give no clue to the origin of the people working inside the store. In fact, they often seem to be run by _____ (**4.**) people from various parts of the globe. Their nationalities often reflect the history of immigration to that country, and they frequently come from nations with a reputation for successful trade and shopkeeping.

But what are the economics of such places? How can tiny shops make any profit when employees have to be paid to work _____ (**5.**) such long hours? _____ (**6.**) answer lies partly with the culture of hard work, but is mainly due to a tradition of employing family. This is very different from the typical American or British family in which the individual members have separate lives and careers. When _____ (**7.**) immigrant family owns a store everyone gets involved—brothers, sisters, uncles, aunts, cousins, grandparents and children—everybody is expected to work behind the counter. Thus, there is _____ (**8.**) guaranteed source of staff available to work from early morning until late at _____ (**9.**) night. And rather than being paid salaries, the members of the family often simply share in _____ (**10.**) profits at the end of the year. It is a recipe that has brought wealth to many immigrant families, and made life a lot easier for those of us who run out of milk at eleven o'clock on a Sunday evening!

b Look at the underlined words. Find words with similar meanings in the article.

Ex: Macy's is a <u>famous</u> department store in New York City. __*well-known*__

1. They just bought a <u>large</u> house. _____
2. People who live in the country are sometimes prejudiced against <u>people who live in a city</u>. _____
3. We <u>hardly ever</u> take vacations. _____
4. The government is considering changing the law on <u>people moving to this country from another one</u>. _____
5. I have never understood the <u>financial basis</u> of international trade. _____
6. The <u>origin</u> of the Nile River is in Uganda. _____

Grammar

3 Fill in the blanks in the article in Exercise 2a with *a*, *an*, *the*, or Ø (the zero article).

4 Ten of these sentences contain mistakes. Correct the mistakes.

_____ 1. Would you prefer milk or cream in your coffee?
_____ 2. Janine and Mike have beautiful garden.
_____ 3. She'd been living in the Los Angeles since the 1980s.
_____ 4. Heathrow is the busiest airport in the United Kingdom.
_____ 5. When I was young, I wanted to be astronaut.
_____ 6. Let's have another look at a first one they showed us.
_____ 7. I think cell phone is the greatest invention ever.
_____ 8. Teresa's first husband was an engineer.
_____ 9. Huan's planning to study the philosophy in college.
_____ 10. Have you got the double room with a sea view?
_____ 11. The Azores are in the middle of Atlantic Ocean.
_____ 12. Geography was my favorite subject in school.
_____ 13. I love looking at a moon at night.
_____ 14. This is most exciting book I've read for a long time.
_____ 15. Vail is one of the most expensive ski resorts in the Rockies.

5 Circle the correct choice.

A: How do you *think/feel* (**1.**) about reality TV shows?

B: You mean things like *Big Brother*?

A: Yes.

B: I think they're quite exciting. What *for/about* (**2.**) you? *How/What* (**3.**) do you think?

A: I think they're awful. They make ordinary people look stupid.

B: Maybe. But isn't it *real/true* (**4.**) that people choose to be on them? Nobody forces them to take part.

A: I suppose so. But *do/are* (**5.**) you agree that TV companies take advantage of people sometimes?

B: Not really. But I think it's important that the people understand what will happen to them afterwards.

A: Yes. You're right. What *more/else* (**6.**) do you think is important?

Reading

1a Read the factfile below about five leading multinational companies. Check (✓) the correct column in the chart.

	Nestlé	Coca-Cola	Zara	Shell	Gap
1. the youngest company					
2. the oldest company					
3. has the most stores					
4. has the highest value of sales					
5. based in San Francisco					
6. founded in London					
7. employs the most people					
8. employs the fewest people					
9. famous for its advertisements					
10. owns businesses in 200 countries					

b Find words in the factfile that mean:

1. drinks (*n.*) _____
2. doesn't include alcohol (*adj.*) _____
3. company that makes products (*n.*) _____
4. eat or drink (*v.*) _____
5. company that takes products to many different locations (*n.*) _____
6. well-known products of a company (*n.*) _____
7. throughout the world (*adj.*) _____
8. started a company or institution (*v.*) _____

Multinational Factfile

Nestlé was founded by Henri Nestlé in 1866. Its headquarters are in Vevey, Switzerland. Nestlé is currently the world's largest manufacturer of food and beverages, with international sales of 110 billion Swiss Francs (122 billion dollars). Nestlé employs 280,000 people all over the world.

Coca-Cola is based in Atlanta, Georgia, USA. Founded in 1886, it is now the world's largest manufacturer and distributor of non-alcoholic beverages, with almost 140,000 employees working in 200 different countries. It is estimated that 50 billion Coca-Cola products are consumed every day. Its sales are worth almost 56 billion dollars per year.

Zara is one of Europe's best known brands of clothing stores. It is part of the Inditex group, based in La Coruña, Spain. The first Zara shop opened in La Coruña in 1975. The group now owns 5,221 stores in 57 countries. Its sales are 7 billion euros (around nine billion dollars) and it employs 47,046 people.

Royal Dutch Shell is a multinational company famous for its gas stations and oil production facilities. Founded by Marcus Samuel in London in 1833, the company merged with the Royal Dutch group in 1907. Shell's international headquarters is now in the Hague, Holland. Shell operates in 90 countries and employs around 100,000 people. Shell generates an income of around 350 billion dollars from its worldwide operations.

Famous for its clothing stores and imaginative advertising campaigns, the Gap is one of the world's most recognizable clothing brands. The first Gap store opened in San Francisco, California, in 1969, and the company is still based in this city. There are now 3,200 Gap stores worldwide, employing 150,000 people. The company achieves sales of around 14 billion dollars annually.

Grammar

2 Rewrite each sentence using the word in parentheses.

Ex: Some of these new computer games are challenging. (incredibly)

Some of these new computer games are
incredibly challenging.

1. When I have a headache, all I want to do is lie down. (bad)

   _____
   _____

2. He didn't work, so he was bound to fail the exam. (hard)

   _____
   _____

3. You're very early; did you drive? (fast)

   _____
   _____

4. Anna is always dressed in designer outfits. (expensively)

   _____
   _____

5. The clients will expect to get a discount. (certainly)

   _____
   _____

6. It snowed during our entire vacation. (heavily)

   _____
   _____

7. He interrupted me in the middle of my speech. (rudely)

   _____
   _____

8. Do you know them? (well)

   _____
   _____

9. I'm going to take the First Aid Certificate exam this year. (definitely)

   _____
   _____

10. The weather can be hot in September. (surprisingly)

    _____
    _____

3 Match the underlined phrases with words and phrases in the box. Some of them are not used.

completely ruined	recently	hard
reasonably priced	hardly	late
unbelievably	nearly	near
probably high	unlikely	well

1. This new computer is <u>not expensive at all</u>.

   _____

2. Our vacation was <u>totally spoiled</u> by the awful weather. _____

3. She hasn't been coming to classes <u>in the last few weeks</u>. _____

4. The class found the exercise <u>difficult</u>.

   _____

5. My uncle speaks Thai <u>fluently</u>.

   _____

6. We'll <u>almost certainly</u> move to the country next year. _____

7. My son is <u>almost</u> six years old now.

   _____

8. Liwei getting a promotion seems <u>hard to believe</u>. _____

9. Sheila handed in her essay <u>after it was due</u>.

   _____

10. The plane flew <u>at a great height</u> over the city.

    _____

Vocabulary

4 Choose the correct words to complete each sentence.

1. Nearly all the students ____ the survey.
   - **a.** took part of
   - **b.** took in
   - **c.** took part in

2. You should never take good health ____ .
   - **a.** for grant
   - **b.** as granted
   - **c.** for granted

3. A Korean company has ____ that old factory.
   - **a.** taken over
   - **b.** taken up
   - **c.** taken out

4. I tried it for a month, but I didn't really ____ that new diet.
   - **a.** take to
   - **b.** take at
   - **c.** take in

5. The use of electric cars has never really ____ in the USA.
   - **a.** taken off
   - **c.** taken out
   - **b.** taken part in

6. It didn't worry me at all, I took ____ .
   - **a.** it in the stride
   - **c.** it all in stride
   - **b.** all in my stride

1 Complete the sentences using the correct form of verbs from the box.

> build   take   invade   play
> start   wait   watch   work

1. Napoleon _____ Russia in 1812.

2. I managed to finish my essay while the children _____ in the back yard.

3. By the time the train arrived, I _____ for more than two hours.

4. I was delayed by the traffic, so when I got to the golf course I found my friends _____ without me.

5. The Egyptians _____ the Great Pyramid about 4,000 years ago.

6. We _____ television when we heard an enormous bang from the street.

7. When he got home, Hiro collapsed onto the sofa, exhausted—he _____ at the factory all day.

8. I _____ a bath when I heard the news on the radio.

2 Circle the correct choice.

Isambard Kingdom Brunel

Isambard Kingdom Brunel was *most/the most/a most* (**1.**) famous British engineer of the 19th century.

Born in 1806 in *a Portsmouth/the Portsmouth/ Portsmouth* (**2.**), his first major work was the construction of a railway between London and Bristol in the west of England. The construction of *a railway/the railway/ railway* (**3.**) involved building *a tunnel/tunnel/the tunnel* (**4.**) near the town of Box, in Somerset. It was three kilometers long, *longest/a longest/the longest* (**5.**) tunnel ever constructed at the time.

After his success with railways, Brunel turned his attention to *the ships/ships* (**6.**). He wanted to connect his railway line in Bristol with New York in *United States/a United States/the United States* (**7.**). In 1838, he built the first large steam-powered ship to cross *the Atlantic/ Atlantic/an Atlantic* (**8.**) in only 15 days.

Brunels' next project was to build *the ship/a ship/ ship* (**9.**) made of iron. He achieved this in 1843 with the "Great Britain." It was also the first to be driven by *a propeller/the propeller* (**10.**).

The ambition/An ambition/Ambition (**11.**) and *the stubbornness/a stubbornness/stubbornness* (**12.**) were the greatest features of Brunel's character; he always tried to design the biggest and best.

3 Complete the crossword.

Across

4. What is the ____ style of dress of your country?

5. I got a job in March, but for the ____ two months I was unemployed.

6. The pyramids are the greatest monuments of ____ Egypt.

8. There was rationing ____ World War II.

9. My grandmother is 81; she's quite ____.

Down

1. Some of my aunt's clothes are very old-____.

2. Up to that ____, I had been an engineer.

3. ____ clothes aren't always expensive.

6. That old hotel is full of beautiful ____ furniture.

7. What will life be like in the 22nd ____?

4 Match each object with a noun or adjective.

____	1. a wedding ring	a. silk
____	2. a mirror	b. rough
____	3. bed sheets	c. denim
____	4. ice on a road	d. gold
____	5. a cushion	e. slippery
____	6. a pair of jeans	f. stretchy
____	7. a wedding dress	g. soft
____	8. a rubber band	h. leather
____	9. a mountain path	i. shiny
____	10. expensive shoes	j. cotton

5 Eight sentences have mistakes. Find and correct the mistakes.

1. Kiri often arrives lately for work.
2. We had to drive slowly because of the heavy rain.
3. I find people around here are general pretty friendly.
4. She's much better; she's feeling finely today.
5. My sister can type fastly.
6. Despite studying hardly, Maria failed the test.
7. Have you seen any good movies recently?
8. I thought that book was more interestingly than the others.
9. Have you ever noticed how highly frogs can jump?
10. This is definite the best restaurant we've been to for ages.

6 Rewrite these sentences with the words in the correct order.

1. The professor/in a friendly way/treats all his students.

   _____

   _____

2. Isabel is/the oldest/definitely/student in our class.

   _____

   _____

3. I washed/this morning/the sheets.

   _____

   _____

4. My brother/forgets/sometimes/his PIN.

   _____

   _____

5. Daniela left/in the corner/of the room/her suitcase.

   _____

   _____

6. The children/forgot/unfortunately/to bring their bathing suits.

   _____

   _____

7. He wasn't/dangerously/driving,/but he was going pretty fast.

   _____

   _____

8. She has a/personality/warm/and caring.

   _____

   _____

7 Circle the correct choice.

1. It's very hard to take _in/out_ all this information.
2. Marco's relaxed about what happened; he took it all in _steps/stride_.
3. Mr. Lester is going to take _under/over_ the Detroit branch.
4. I'm taking part _in/at_ a demonstration against the war.
5. Dan took _at/to_ his fiancée's parents as soon as he met them.
6. Playing soccer has never really taken _out/off_ in the US.

8 Rewrite the sentences. Replace the phrases in _italics_ with nouns. Make other changes as needed.

Ex: She _writes books for a living_.
   She is a writer.

1. Sun-Yi _loves being a mother_.

   _____

2. _Having friends_ is the most important thing for Pepe.

   _____

3. David _plays the piano professionally_.

   _____

4. We need to increase _the amount we produce_.

   _____

5. _Being happy_ is more important than wealth.

   _____

6. I'm not very pleased with the _thing you arranged_.

   _____

7. Professor Grant _invents things_.

   _____

8. Children love _feeling excited_.

   _____

9. There is a lot of crime in this _place where neighbors live_.

   _____

10. My brother _makes a living studying physics_.

   _____

Reading

1a Read the newspaper article and choose the best title.

1. Newspapers' Deadly Rival
2. Blogging Websites
3. The Internet News Millionaire

b Read the article again. Mark the sentences true (*T*) or false (*F*).

____ 1. Drudge calls himself "the ultimate blogger."

____ 2. He loved news and current affairs even as a child.

____ 3. He was a journalist for *The Washington Star*.

____ 4. The Internet didn't exist when Drudge was a child.

____ 5. Drudge got his news from talking to people.

____ 6. He interviewed Monica Lewinsky in 1998.

____ 7. The *Drudge Report* is very useful for people who want up-to-date news.

____ 8. Matt Drudge doesn't think the Internet will take over from newspapers in the future.

c Find these phrases in the article and match them with their meanings.

____ 1. sprung up (paragraph 1)

____ 2. stems from (paragraph 2)

____ 3. obsession (paragraph 2)

____ 4. dead-end jobs (paragraph 2)

____ 5. sifting through (paragraph 3)

____ 6. juiciest gossip (paragraph 3)

____ 7. breaking news (paragraph 3)

____ 8. news-junkie (paragraph 4)

a. things that are happening now

b. someone who wants to know the latest news all the time

c. looking very carefully at all the details to find something

d. an overriding interest in something

e. began *or* originated with

f. work that has no future and doesn't lead to a career

g. appeared from nowhere

h. exciting or shocking scandal

① This is Matt Drudge, millionaire founder and owner of the *Drudge Report*, the first and most successful online "newspaper." People have called Drudge the ultimate blogger but he doesn't accept the description. He considers the *Drudge Report* to be a real newspaper, very different from the thousands of blogs that have sprung up on the Internet.

② Drudge's fascination for news and gossip stems from a childhood job delivering papers for *The Washington Star*. It gave him plenty of time and opportunity to catch up with the latest news. Uninterested in school work or sports, Drudge developed an obsession with rumors and political gossip. In school, his only good subject was Current Affairs. Following a series of dead-end jobs, Drudge ended up in Los Angeles in the 1990s, just in time for the beginning of what was to become the Internet.

③ The early internet was a fertile hunting ground for Drudge. He spent hours sifting through the newsgroups and the websites that existed then, searching for rumors and inside stories from the political and entertainment worlds. He launched the *Drudge Report* website in 1995, a daily "rumor bulletin" containing his version of the latest and juiciest gossip from Hollywood and Washington. Always managing to be the first with breaking news, Drudge's success was assured when he became the first person to publicize the Monica Lewinsky scandal in 1998.

④ Now with revenue of over $1 million a year and many thousands of subscribers, the *Drudge Report* has become a "must read" resource for those hungry for the latest news and gossip. But will the ever-increasing availability of news on the Internet mean the end for its older rival, the conventional newspaper? Drudge doesn't think so. He sees the two working together. As far as news-junkie Drudge is concerned, there can never be too much news.

Grammar

2 Rewrite the sentences using conditionals. Start each sentence with *If*. Be careful with modal verbs.

Real conditional

Ex: I hope he asks me to marry him because I would accept.

If he asks me to marry him, I'll accept.

1. I'm planning to get a laptop so I can send emails when I'm traveling.

   _____

2. I don't want to be late for my interview so I hope the train comes on time.

   _____

3. Maribel hopes to pass the driving test because she wants to buy a car.

   _____

Present unreal conditional

Ex: The government wants to build more roads but they don't have enough money.

If the government had more money, it would build more roads.

4. I'd like to swim more often but I don't live near a pool.

   _____

5. Terry would like to travel around the world but he's scared of flying.

   _____

6. Celia's dream is to join a choir but unfortunately she can't sing.

   _____

Past unreal conditional

Ex: I met him because I went to the movie theater.

If I hadn't gone to the movie theater, I wouldn't have met him.

7. Dave won the prize because he knew all the answers.

   _____

8. Sumiko didn't go to the concert because she lost the tickets.

   _____

9. Kasem might have got a promotion but his sales figures were disappointing.

   _____

10. We had to stand in line for tickets so we missed the start of the show.

    _____

3 Complete the conversation using the correct forms of the verbs in parentheses.

Ann: Excuse me. I _____ (**1.** like) to report a stolen purse.

Officer: Of course, ma'am. Let me take some details. Your name?

Ann: Ms. Ann Kendall.

Officer: And where and when did this happen?

Ann: At Rowe's department store, about 20 minutes ago. I put my purse down while I was paying at the counter . . .

Officer: And someone took your purse?

Ann: Exactly. If I'd been paying attention, it _____ (**2.** not happen).

Officer: Any idea who did it?

Ann: Not really. If anyone _____ (**3.** look) suspicious, I would have noticed.

Officer: Were there any security cameras there?

Ann: I don't think so. I'm sure they _____ (**4.** tell) me if they had any.

Officer: And what was in the purse?

Ann: Everything. My cell phone, keys . . .

Officer: Any credit cards?

Ann: Yes, one. The thief might try to use it.

Officer: Well, if you _____ (**5.** phone) your credit card company now, you _____ (**6.** be able) to cancel the cards before anyone can use them.

Ann: OK. But what about my keys? The thief might be able to get into my house.

Officer: Was there anything in your bag that had your address on it, like a driver's license?

Ann: No, I don't think so.

Officer: Well, don't worry. If the thief _____ (**7.** not have) your address, he _____ (**8.** not know) where you live.

Ann: No, I suppose not. Do you think there's any chance of getting my purse back?

Officer: It's hard to say, but if anybody _____ (**9.** find) it, we _____ (**10.** contact) you.

Writing

4 Imagine you are a famous person. Write a 100 word blog about an exciting day in your life on a separate sheet of paper. Use these questions and page 46 of the Student Book to help you.

- Where were you? Why were you there?
- What happened? What time did it happen?
- How do you feel about what happened?

Vocabulary

1 Circle the correct answer.

1. I love to roast hotdogs over a fire when I'm *camping/kayaking*.

2. Make sure to *take in/pitch* your tent on a flat surface.

3. When Paul goes rock climbing, he always brings a *harness/handhold*.

4. She told me that the *view/whitewater rafting* from the top of the mountain looks amazing. She wanted to sit on the grass and enjoy it forever.

5. This kayak costs $275, and comes with *rapids/a paddle*.

6. Yumi's *rope/summit* broke while she was rappelling. Luckily, she wasn't injured.

Writing

2 Read the article on how to change a flat tire. Summarize the information and rewrite it as instructions. Use imperatives and short sentences.

Ex: • Stop the car.
   • Put on the handbrake.

How to change a flat tire

Getting a puncture in one of your car's tires can be very annoying, and it's dangerous to attempt to drive a car that has a flat tire. Luckily, changing the tire is really pretty easy. First of all, you should stop the car and make sure the handbrake is on. Then, look in the trunk of the car and find the spare tire, take it out, and put it on the ground. Then take out the jack and the wrench—they're usually in a bag somewhere in the trunk.

If your wheel has a hubcap, you should remove it. Using the wrench, slightly loosen each nut (one full turn counter-clockwise). Now, you are ready to raise the car off the ground. Carefully position the jack (your car owner's manual will tell you where you need to place it) and gradually raise the car about 4 inches, or 10 centimeters, off the ground by turning the handle on the jack.

Next, use the wrench to completely unscrew the nuts on the wheel. After removing the nuts, you'll be able to pull the wheel off. Don't forget to put it in the trunk so you can take it to be repaired later. Now you lift up the spare wheel and slip it into position, put the nuts back and tighten them up by hand—don't use the wrench.

Once you've done that, you can lower the car back on to the ground. Now, it's time to really tighten the nuts—so use the wrench and turn the nuts clockwise as hard as you can. Replace the hubcap if you've got one. Make sure you've put the jack, the wrench, and the old wheel back in the trunk and you're ready to go!

wheel

tire

nuts

jack (with handle)

wrench

Reading and Grammar

3a Read the conversation between Pilar and her great grandfather. Answer the questions on a separate piece of paper.

Pilar:	Come on Great Grandpa, smile. I want to take your photo.
Grandpa:	OK Pilar, but where's the camera?
Pilar:	This is a camera.
Grandpa:	I thought that was a cell phone.
Pilar:	Well, yes, but you _____ (1.) have a special camera to take photos these days; you can use your phone.
Grandpa:	Amazing! _____ (2.) I go over to the window where there's more light?
Pilar:	No, no, you _____ (3.) do that. It has a flash.
Grandpa:	Oh, OK. Well, I'm ready.
Pilar:	Um, you _____ (4.) put your hand there. I can't see your face.
Grandpa:	Oh. OK.
Pilar:	Great. Oh, that didn't turn out very well; it's a little out of focus. I think I'm _____ (5.) further away from you.
Grandpa:	How do you know it's out of focus? _____ (6.) take it for the film to be developed?
Pilar:	Of course not, it's digital! You can see the picture right away.
Grandpa:	Oh, "digital," of course. Cameras have certainly changed since I was young!
Pilar:	In the 1950s? Didn't you have cameras then?
Grandpa:	No. There were plenty of cameras around. But you _____ (7.) use film and then you had to take it in to a store to get it processed and made into prints.
Pilar:	Boring.
Grandpa:	Not really. It was exciting waiting for the prints to come back.
Pilar:	Oh, I wouldn't want to wait.
Grandpa:	Well, Pilar, you _____ (8.) be so impatient. Everything comes to those who wait!
Pilar:	I know, but I like things to be instant. Anyway, let me take another picture of you.
Grandpa:	Actually, I'm a little tired now, Pilar. Can we do it later?
Pilar:	OK, Great Grandpa!

1. What is Pilar using?
2. What does her great grandfather do with his hand?
3. Why isn't Pilar's photo a success?
4. Why is Pilar's great grandfather confused?
5. What was different about taking photos in the 1950s?

b Who says it? Write Pilar (*P*) or Great Grandpa (*G*).

____ 1. . . . you can use your phone.
____ 2. It has a flash.
____ 3. How do you know . . . ?
____ 4. There were plenty of cameras around.
____ 5. . . . I like things to be instant.

c Now read the conversation again. Complete the conversation using the words in the box. Some words will be used more than once.

don't need to	should	had to
supposed to be	shouldn't	
don't you have to	don't have to	

d Find these words in the conversation.

1. Two other nouns that mean *photo*.
   _____
2. Two verbs that describe a procedure involving chemicals. _____
3. A noun that means *the part of a camera that makes a bright light*. _____
4. A three-word expression that means *blurred* or *not clear*. _____
5. An adjective that has a similar meaning to *electronic*. _____

4 Six sentences have mistakes. Find and correct the mistakes.

1. You're soaking wet. You should have gone out in the rain!
2. We should hurry; there isn't much time left.
3. Don't worry. You can't pay to get in—it's free.
4. Must you wear a school uniform when you were a child?
5. We really should buy one of those new MP3 players. They're excellent.
6. In some countries, you should get a license to use a TV—it's the law.
7. Excuse me. You don't have to smoke in here. It isn't allowed.
8. I'm not surprised you failed the test; you shouldn't have done more work.

Reading

1a Read the ad and choose the best answer.
In general, who is the ad aimed at? ____

    a. people who play extreme sports

    b. people who might like to try extreme sports

    c. people who want to improve their physical fitness

b Read the ad again. Answer the questions on a separate piece of paper.

    1. How many extreme sports are mentioned by name within the text in the ad?

    2. What two things can you get from the website?

    3. Is the weekend suitable for people who aren't physically fit?

    4. How many extreme sports were available last year?

    5. How much do tickets cost if you buy them at the event itself?

c Find words or phrases in the ad that mean:

    1. boring, always the same (*adj.*) _____

    2. when you know what will happen in advance (*adj.*) _____

    3. having a strong desire to do something (*phr. v.*) _____

    4. an opportunity to make something imaginary come true (*phrase*) _____

    5. extremely exciting (*adj.*) _____

    6. most important and knowledgeable (*adj.*) _____

    7. well-protected (*compound adj.*) _____

    8. teachers of physical skills (*n.*) _____

How much danger can you take?
Join us for *National Extreme Sports Weekend* and find out!

- Have you ever watched snowboarders and mountain bikers and thought, "I could do that"?
- Are you tired of the humdrum daily routine and ready to challenge yourself?
- Are you longing for some real risk in your predictable everyday life?

Well, now is your chance to turn fantasy into thrilling reality . . .

This year, *National Extreme Sports Weekend* is better than ever. We are offering you the chance to try out over 50 different extreme sports, twice as many as previous years. 100 leading instructors from around the world are waiting to share their top tips and closely-guarded secrets. And you don't even need to be in great shape; we have something for everyone!

rappelling   *bungee jumping*   *kayaking*

skateboarding   *in-line skating*

snowboarding

whitewater rafting   *hang gliding*

Are you ready for the risk of a lifetime? Are you ready for the challenge?
If you don't come, you'll never know!

National Extreme Sports Weekend is at Fairfield Park, Seattle, July 21—22.
Tickets and a full schedule of events available from www.NatExsports.com.
$20 at the event, $15 in advance.

Grammar

2 Rewrite these sentences using the correct form of *do* to make them emphatic.

1. I like your new suit.

   _____

2. Amanda complains a lot.

   _____

3. He said he was sorry several times.

   _____

4. I asked the boss for permission.

   _____

5. We know what we are talking about.

   _____

3 Circle the correct choice.

1. I *such/really* didn't understand what she was saying.
2. Their new house was *so/just* expensive.
3. The cotton suit is *much/such*, much cheaper than the silk one.
4. *Million Dollar Baby* was *such/so* a good movie.
5. It's a *such/very*, very good hotel.
6. Clint Eastwood is *such/just* fantastic in that role.
7. His sister is *so/such* beautiful, don't you agree?
8. This new artist is *very/really*, really talented.

4 Rewrite the sentences to emphasize the underlined words. Begin each sentence with *It*.

   Ex: I can't stand her new boyfriend.
   It's her new boyfriend that I can't stand.

1. They love Chinese food.

   _____

2. She spoke to his assistant.

   _____

3. I didn't like the first movie.

   _____

4. My thumb hurts, not my finger.

   _____

5. Clara really doesn't like modern poetry.

   _____

6. I really don't understand his attitude.

   _____

Vocabulary

5a Circle the correct choice.

1. I wasn't able to *find/give* out what time the movie starts.
2. You'll have to use another printer. This one's *run/sorted* out of ink.
3. It was hard work but it *fell/turned* out all right in the end.
4. Mel, please *pass/take* out a copy to everyone in class 3C.
5. Jim's going to *sort/find* out the files.

b Four of these sentences have mistakes. Find and correct them.

1. We weren't sure about the babysitter, but she took out to be really good.
2. Dan's had to go to the gym on his own since he found out that his gym partner is on vacation.
3. My car broke down last week and the mechanic wasn't able to put it out.
4. I'm afraid we only pass out catalogs to established clients.
5. Make sure you fall out your cigarette before you enter the building.
6. If I have a problem with my house, my neighbor turns it out—he's a construction manager.

6 Compare and contrast the photos. Write about 150 words on a separate sheet of paper. Mention:

- two things that are the same
- two things that are different
- speculations about the situations
- your own reactions and opinions

1 Complete the sentences with words from the box. Some of the words are not used.

> ambition   substantial   hardly   vast
> gamble   incredibly   luck
> dream   opportunity   stake

1. To be successful in business you need a lot of _____ .

2. Although I knew it was a _____ , I invested all my money in my best friend's new store.

3. I'm sorry you didn't win. I hope you have better _____ next time.

4. When I was a child it was my _____ to become an astronaut.

5. Our company lost a lot of money this year so our jobs are at _____ .

6. You should never swim during a thunderstorm; it's _____ dangerous.

7. I'm very glad that I had the _____ to travel when I was young.

2 Circle the correct form of the verbs to complete the sentences.

1. I ____ by taxi if I were you.
   a. 'd go   **b.** must go   **c.** 'll go

2. If you ____ some ice in a drink, it makes it cooler.
   a. have put   **b.** put   **c.** will put

3. I ____ for the movie if you pay for the restaurant.
   a. paid   **b.** 'll pay   **c.** am paying

4. If you ____ a positive attitude, you won't succeed in business.
   a. don't have   **b.** didn't have   **c.** haven't had

5. What ____ if your car broke down on the freeway?
   a. will you do   **c.** are you doing
   b. would you do

6. If Steven hadn't passed the exam, he ____ to college.
   a. didn't go   **c.** wouldn't go
   b. wouldn't have gone

7. They ____ that hotel if they'd known how expensive it was.
   a. didn't choose   **c.** wouldn't choose
   b. wouldn't have chosen

3 Match the pictures with the words or phrases in the box. Some choices are not used.

> rock climbing   kayaking   swing
> taking in the view   rappelling   tuck
> pitching a tent   camping

1. _____

2. _____

3. _____

4. _____

5. _____

6. _____

4 Circle the correct choice.

1. In Australia you *must/need to* drive on the left; that's the law.

2. You *can't/needn't* use cell phones while a plane is taking off or landing.

3. You're covered in mud. You *shouldn't/mustn't* have been playing in the garden!

4. I *was supposed to/must* be there by six, but I missed my bus.

5. She's been so helpful. Do you think I *have to/should* take her a bunch of flowers?

6. Don't worry; we *shouldn't/don't have* to stay very long.

7. We *didn't have to/should have* asked for permission before we borrowed her keys.

8. I feel very guilty—I *should/don't have to* apologize to him.

9. The doctor is very busy, so you *can't/don't have to* be late for the appointment.

10. You *'re supposed to/didn't have to* bring soap; the hotel supplies it free of charge.

5 Complete the sentences with the correct phrasal verbs.

1. Karl goes to the gym every day and _____ out.

2. Although the heat was intense, the firefighters managed to _____ out the fire.

3. Excuse me, Alex. Could you _____ out the time of the next train to Osaka?

4. Can you get me a few things at the supermarket? We've _____ out of bread, coffee and milk.

5. Don't worry about cleaning up—I'll help you _____ out the mess.

6 Put the words in the correct order to make emphatic sentences.

Ex: that/the children/go there/It/want to/is
    It is the children that want to go there.

1. made me/It was/feel sick/that/the shellfish
    _____
    _____

2. try/She/you/did/to contact
    _____
    _____

3. really,/do volunteer work/I/who /really/ admire people
    _____
    _____

4. I/It/my/injured/is/left leg/that
    _____
    _____

5. such a/soccer player/Min-sook/good/is
    _____
    _____

6. money/give/Carla/a lot of/to charity/does
    _____
    _____

7. that/It/cell phone/was stolen/was/my
    _____
    _____

8. expensive/very,/My/was/new computer/very
    _____
    _____

9. do/Javier/did/work/a lot of/for us
    _____
    _____

10. does/the housework/It/his wife/is/that/ most of
    _____
    _____

7 Complete the sentences with words from the box.

that	so	such	is
does	did	really	it

1. It's John's children _____ I feel sorry for.

2. I think Sylvia really _____ love him.

3. Monet's paintings are really, _____ beautiful.

4. _____ was Elizabeth I was trying to contact.

5. I _____ try to get front row seats but they were sold out.

6. That flat screen television is _____ expensive.

7. Thanh is _____ a wonderful mother.

8. It _____ the final episode I want you to record.

LESSON 1

Communication

1a Read the interview.

The Melting Pot
by Sanjay Roy

Anyone who has seen a commercial for athletic gear is familiar with the work of British director Joe Grindel. Now, he's working on feature films in Hollywood. Earlier this week, I sat down with Joe to discuss the twists and turns of his career.

J: Yeah. I came here when I was 28.

S: What made you choose to live in the States?

J: Well, work really. I had a reasonably successful career back in London, making TV commercials and short films, but I really wanted to get into feature films.

S: You made those famous commercials for running shoes, didn't you?

J: Yes. I _____ (1.) do lots of work for sportswear companies. Some studio executives saw my work and invited me to Hollywood.

S: Were you always interested in making movies?

J: I guess so. When I was a child I _____ (2.) spend hours watching Hollywood movies on TV. My parents gave me a movie camera when I was about ten. I _____ (3.) drive the family crazy filming everything!

S: You've made three movies over here now. How does film-making here compare to the UK?

J: There's a lot more money involved. Back in the UK, we _____ (4.) have much contact with the accountants. But here they're on top of you all the time!

S: Do you find that difficult?

J: Well, let's just say I'm still _____ (5.) it!

S: Is there anything you really miss from the old country?

J: For me, no. But my wife misses walking to the stores. The distances between places are enormous here. In London, we had lots of local stores so we _____ (6.) usually walk to get our groceries.

S: Yes. Nobody walks here. They go to the gym instead!

J: I know. People drive to the gym and then spend hours walking on the treadmills. Crazy!

S: Any trouble understanding the American accent . . .

J: Oh, I _____ (7.) that. It's probably more difficult for you guys to understand me. Although I can't say I've really had any problems.

b Complete the notes in the chart.

Work	US: *Joe makes feature films.* UK: (1.) _____
Movie-making	US: (2.) _____ UK: (3.) _____
Shopping	US: (4.) _____ UK: (5.) _____

c Read the interview again and write the questions for these answers.

Ex: About ten.

  How old was Joe when his parents gave
  him a movie camera?

1. Five years.
   _____
   _____

2. Twenty-eight.
   _____
   _____

3. Work.
   _____
   _____

4. There is more money involved.
   _____
   _____

5. Walking to the stores.
   _____
   _____

d Read the interview one more time. Find the words in the reading that mean:

1. when people from many backgrounds mix together _____

2. managers of movie companies _____

3. do something that irritates people _____

4. constantly supervising and watching somebody _____

Grammar

2 Look at the interview in Exercise 1 again. Complete the interview using appropriate forms of *used to*, *get used to* or *would*.

Vocabulary

3 Complete the crossword with words to describe appearance.

Across

2. models are this way so they can fit into small sizes
3. not tall, but strong and thick
5. the opposite of straight hair
8. having no hair
10. looking untidy or a little shabby
11. graceful and attractive
12. looking like someone who works out at the gym a lot

Down

1. hair that is short and sticks up in sharp points
4. a little fat
6. you're like this if you sunbathe and your skin becomes darker
7. older people have these on their faces
9. not a natural hair color

4 Cross out the forms that are NOT possible in each sentence. Some may have more than one answer.

1. When I was a child I ____ play soccer all the time.
   a. would   b. got used to   c. used to
2. Gerald ____ be overweight.
   a. used to   b. would   c. didn't use to
3. Our youngest child ____ watch television for hours on end.
   a. would   b. used to   c. was used to
4. It took me a long time to ____ this new diet.
   a. get use to   c. getting used to
   b. get used to
5. ____ that new computer?
   a. Are you getting used to   c. Are you used to
   b. Do you get used to
6. Do you think she ____ living on her own?
   a. gets used to   c. is used to
   b. will get used to

Writing

5a Use the photos to complete the chart.

	Jennifer	Tim
Age		
Face		
Hair		
Build		
Clothes		

b Use the information to write a short description of each person on a separate piece of paper.

Tim

Jennifer

Reading

1a Read the short story quickly and circle the best title.

   a. The Burglar from Texas

   b. Driving in Monterrey

   c. The Disastrous Vacation

Melody and Josh were very excited about going to Mexico on vacation. They packed their new convertible with three suitcases and set off from their home in Texas early in the morning. The weather was warm, and as they drove across the border into Mexico, they lowered the roof of the car and enjoyed the pleasant sensation of the warm spring air rushing past their heads.

By the middle of the afternoon, they had reached the town of Monterrey. Melody _____ (**1.**) map-reading, but she was sure they _____ (**2.**) make their way to the center of the city, find a parking space, and enjoy a delicious, late lunch at a local restaurant. As they drove further into the city, they suddenly heard a loud bang, and felt something crash into the back of their car. Turning around, they saw a small motorcycle lying on its side behind their car with two young men sprawled on the road beside it. Josh stopped the car and jumped out to see if he _____ (**3.**) help. One of the young men was groaning loudly. Melody _____ (**4.**) give first aid, so she opened her door and approached the groaning man. Suddenly, the two men jumped up and rushed towards the Mercedes. In less than two seconds, they had leaped into the car and driven off at high speed, leaving Josh and Melody standing in the street.

Josh started shouting for help in English. But there was nobody around to hear him. At first, Melody wasn't too worried. She _____ (**5.**) speak Spanish either, but she was sure they'd _____ (**6.**) find a police station nearby. After half an hour of walking, they had still failed to find a police officer or anyone to help them and they began to get more worried. Their passports, credit cards, cell phones and money had all been in the car, and Josh was worried that the thieves might be using his credit cards to go on a huge spending spree.

About twenty minutes later, they saw a police car driving along the street and they rushed into the road to flag it down. Josh tried to explain what had happened to the police officer. But the officer _____ (**7.**) understand English and decided to take the two tourists back to the police station. He was sure one of his co-workers would _____ (**8.**) translate for them. Unfortunately, as he was driving back to the police station, there was an emergency call on his radio and he was instructed to drive to the scene of a serious accident. Josh and Melody were forced to sit in the back of the police car for another two hours while the officer dealt with the emergency.

By the time they arrived at the local police station, it was eight o'clock in the evening and they were exhausted. Using the police station's phone, Josh _____ (**9.**) contacting his credit card company to cancel his cards. Once they'd done this, they decided the best thing was to get home as quickly as possible. A police officer drove them to the bus station and loaned them the money to buy two tickets. They just had time to catch the last bus — the slow, overnight service back across the border to Texas.

Relieved to be on their way home, the couple soon fell asleep. They woke at seven in the morning as the bus pulled into the border station, where they _____ (**10.**) change buses, and then rode for another four hours until they reached their hometown. With no money for a taxi, they were forced to walk for several miles to their house. Just as they finally turned down their street, they saw a large moving van leaving. Melody was surprised; she didn't think any of their neighbors were moving. As they approached their house, they noticed the front door was open. Running into the house, Josh gasped with shock. The house was completely empty. Then, he remembered. Their house keys had been on the same ring as the car key . . .

b Complete the story on the previous page using the words from the box.

> couldn't (x2)   be able to   could (x2)
> knew how to   manage to
> succeeded in   managed to
> wasn't very good at

c Read the story again and number events 1–12 in the correct order.

____ Two men drive off in their convertible.

____ They have to wait while the police officer deals with an accident.

____ They catch the slow bus back to Texas.

_1_ Melody and Josh leave their home in Texas.

____ They get into a Mexican police car.

____ Josh and Melody get back to their house in Texas.

____ They get out of their car to see what has happened.

____ The thieves steal everything from their house and drive away in a truck.

____ They walk around trying to find a police station.

____ The police take Melody and Josh to the bus station.

____ They drive into the suburbs of Monterrey.

____ A motorcycle crashes into the back of their car.

d Find words and phrases in the story that mean:

1. a car with a roof that opens (*adj.* or *n.*) _____

2. left on a journey (*phr. v.*) _____

3. moving quickly (*v.*) _____

4. lying with the legs and arms spread out (*v.*) _____

5. making noises, as if in pain (*v.*) _____

6. spending a large amount of money at one time (*phrase*) _____

7. signal a car or taxi to stop (*phr. v.*) _____

8. very tired (*adj.*) _____

9. gave something to somebody, but they have to repay it later (*v.*) _____

10. a large vehicle used to move furniture (*n.*) _____

Grammar

2 Complete each sentence with one word.

1. I'm afraid we weren't _____ to get you any tickets.

2. Did you _____ in getting a pay raise?

3. If they get here on time, they'll _____ able to see the fireworks.

4. I'm terrible _____ cooking, so I eat out most nights.

5. _____ you ride a bicycle when you were a child?

6. Monica's really _____ at languages; she speaks three or four fluently.

7. My uncle _____ to get me a job in his office last summer.

8. Excuse me. Do you know _____ to open this window?

9. At the end of the class you _____ be able to take the exam for the diploma.

10. Don't ask Mi-ra to navigate—she's _____ at map reading.

3 Look at the photo and read the passage. Use the photo to find four mistakes and correct them.

This photo really brings back memories of my childhood vacations with our grandparents. We used to go to the beach in the summer. Although the weather was often very cold, I remember that we had a lot of fun. My two brothers would spend hours fishing in the sea and playing games on the beach. Our family often had picnics there. We would sit in the car and eat sandwiches that my mother had packed for us. It's funny, but those sandwiches always tasted better than the sandwiches we ate at home. Yes, I often get very nostalgic for those days when I see photos of the beach.

Vocabulary

1 Match the statements with the adjectives in the box.

> annoyed   curious   suspicious
> relieved   shocked   optimistic

> Thank goodness you're safe. I was so worried about you!

1. _____

> I wonder what's in that box? I'd love to have a look inside.

2. _____

> I really feel like the interview went well! I think I'll get the job.

3. _____

> His behavior really gets on my nerves. He's so rude!

4. _____

> I don't trust our new boss. I'm sure he wants to get rid of me.

5. _____

> You spent over $500 on a single pair of shoes? That's outrageous!

6. _____

2 Circle the correct choice.

1. The children got very *excited/curious* when I told them we were going to Disneyland next summer.

2. I'll get a good grade; I'm always *optimistic/uneasy* about tests.

3. Chung's very *relieved/uneasy* about making the presentation—the idea of standing up in front of a group of people always worries him.

4. They're really *excited/suspicious* about their new neighbor. He seems to do a lot of strange things in the middle of the night.

5. We were very *relieved/shocked* when we heard that nobody had been hurt in the car crash.

Reading

3a Read the newspaper article. Complete the article with the information below. Write the letter in the blank. Some choices are not used.

The Musician with no Memory

Police in England have appealed for help in identifying a mystery man who was found wandering on a beach two days ago.

The mystery man seems unable to speak, write or understand English. When he was picked up by the police he was nicely dressed in a suit and tie, _____ (**1.**) It had been raining and his clothes were soaking wet. _____ (**2.**) He is white and in his 20s or early 30s.

_____ (**3.**) and put under the supervision of Michael Camp, a local social worker. The mystery deepened when nurses at the hospital gave the man a pen and paper and, _____ (**4.**), he drew a picture of a grand piano. There is a piano in the hospital's chapel, and Mr. Camp took the man there. _____ (**5.**) Onlookers described his performance as "virtuoso." Staff at the hospital dubbed him "The Piano Man."

Police believe the man may be a professional musician who is suffering from amnesia after some kind of traumatic accident. _____ (**6.**) Photos and a description of the man have been circulated around Europe's police forces.

Anyone who thinks they may be able to identify this man is asked to get in touch with the National Missing Persons Helpline.

a. The man was taken to Medway Maritime Hospital

b. Others think he may be a con artist or an illegal immigrant from Eastern Europe.

c. The man was taken to the local hospital, however.

d. He proceeded to sit down and play classical music for two hours non-stop.

e. rather than writing his name and address

f. but the labels were missing, and he had no documents on him.

g. Nevertheless, he is probably not British.

h. Although he did not have any obvious injuries, the man seemed confused and disoriented.

b Complete the sentences using the cues in parentheses and information from the article.

1. He was _____, but his clothes _____. (dressed/ soaking wet)

2. Although he _____, the missing man _____. (speak/play piano)

3. He was _____. However, the _____. (suit/labels)

4. He had no _____. Nevertheless, he _____. (injuries/confused)

5. Though he can't _____, he _____. (words/ pictures)

6. He may _____. However, the police _____. (illegal immigrant/musician)

c Match these words and phrases from the article with their meanings below.

_____ 1. appealed   _____ 6. dubbed

_____ 2. wandering   _____ 7. virtuoso

_____ 3. disoriented   _____ 8. amnesia

_____ 4. chapel   _____ 9. traumatic

_____ 5. non-stop   _____ 10. con artist

a. gave someone a special name

b. someone who makes money tricking people

c. an illness in which you lose your memory

d. asked for assistance

e. extremely stressful

f. confused about where you are

g. continuously

h. walking around without a purpose

i. showing the highest level of skill and talent

j. a room for religious ceremonies

Grammar

4 Complete the sentences with a linking word from the box. Use each linking word once.

Ex: Francesca has a lot of money. She lives in a small apartment.

Although Francesca has a lot of money, she lives in a small apartment.

however	although	but
although	nevertheless	

1. I love vegetables _____ I hate fruit.

2. Your bank account has money in it. _____, we are unable to authorize the loan.

3. _____ there was a lot of rain, a lot of the plants died.

4. We spent two hours at the museum. _____, we forgot to look at the Impressionist paintings.

5 Each sentence has a punctuation and/or word order mistake. Rewrite the sentences correctly.

1. The children we met were healthy. But, very badly educated.

   _____
   _____

2. I've been to New York, although, I've never seen the Statue of Liberty.

   _____
   _____

3. Your visa has expired, nevertheless. We are prepared to allow you to stay for a further three months.

   _____
   _____

4. I hear British Columbia is great for skiing vacations though. I've never been there myself.

   _____
   _____

5. I've lived even though in Chicago for four years, I still get lost on the subway system.

   _____
   _____

6. My grandparents were poor, but, happy.

   _____
   _____

7. Although we enjoy long walks. We do find them quite tiring.

   _____
   _____

8. Pets are not usually allowed in the hotel however. In this case we can make an exception.

   _____
   _____

1 Choose the correct word to complete each sentence.

1. As he gets older, he's getting more and more ____. It's so sad.

   a. forgettable **b.** forgetful **c.** forgetting

2. I get really ____ when I look at these old photos.

   a. remembering **b.** nostalgic **c.** nostalgia

3. ____ me, what was the name of your first boyfriend?

   a. Remember **b.** Remind **c.** Reminisce

4. Do you ____ when we used to go to the beach?

   a. remind **b.** memory **c.** remember

5. My grandparents love to ____ about the old days.

   a. reminisce **b.** nostalgic **c.** remind

6. The fantastic atmosphere made the trip really ____.

   a. memory **b.** memorable **c.** nostalgia

2 Rewrite the sentences using the words in parentheses.

1. Are you becoming accustomed to life in the big city? (getting)

   _____

2. Isabel didn't have any friends when she was a child. (use)

   _____

3. I went to the library every morning when I was a student. (would)

   _____

4. The company doesn't export cars to Asia any longer. (used)

   _____

5. Did he become familiar with the software quickly? (get)

   _____

6. When I was young, I didn't watch much television. (use)

   _____

7. How often did you take the bus to school? (would)

   _____

8. I've become accustomed to staying up late. (gotten)

   _____

3 Replace the words in parentheses with the correct word to complete the sentences.

1. Derek is _____ (he doesn't have a beard) and has blond hair.

2. Mrs. Arkwright is 85, and her face is covered in _____ (lines).

3. When he was young, Jason had a full head of hair, but now I'm afraid he's _____ (got no hair on his head).

4. My brother started doing bodybuilding a few years ago and now he's very _____ (has lots of muscles).

5. Even when he wears suits, Hiro manages to look somewhat _____ (untidy).

6. To be successful in Hollywood you usually have to be _____ (handsome or pretty).

7. I thought Daniela's hair was naturally blond but in fact it's _____ (artificially colored).

8. She has a small _____ (shaped like the letter "O") face and thick dark hair.

4 Complete the sentences using expressions of ability and the verbs in parentheses.

Ex: Young-soon _____ (not eat or drink) for two hours after the operation.
   Young-soon *won't be able to eat or drink* for two hours after the operation.

1. David _____ (repair) his computer after he had spoken to the technician.

2. When I was a young child I _____ (play) soccer for hours without getting tired.

3. The children _____ (not come) on vacation with us next summer.

4. My husband is really _____ (cook) but he's hopeless at cleaning.

5. _____ (you/find) their website on the Internet yesterday?

6. By the end of the class you _____ (type) thirty words a minute.

5 Complete the crossword with adjectives.

Across

1. how you feel when you're somewhat angry or irritated
5. how you feel when you think someone is hiding something bad
6. how you feel when you want to find out about something that interests you

Down

2. how you feel when you think something positive is going to happen
3. how you feel when you're slightly worried and not relaxed
4. how you feel when something you were worried about turns out to be OK
5. how you feel when you see or hear something you weren't expecting or prepared for

6 Choose the best ending or response for each sentence.

1. Although she had flown many times,
   a. Sumiko flew quite often.
   b. Sumiko was still scared of flying.
2. You failed to pass the entrance test.
   a. Nevertheless, we are prepared to allow you to enter the class.
   b. Even though we are prepared to allow you to enter in the class.
3. I wanted to buy a new laptop,
   a. but all the models I looked at were too expensive.
   b. nevertheless all the models were too expensive.
4. The store wouldn't give us a refund,
   a. although they didn't agree to pay for repairs.
   b. although they did agree to pay for repairs.
5. Although I found him boring,
   a. I tried to make conversation with him.
   b. I didn't bother to make conversation with him.
6. Buying first class tickets was more expensive.
   a. However, we thought it was worth it.
   b. But we thought it was worth it.
7. We realize that the package was in good condition when you sent it.
   a. Nevertheless, it was damaged when it arrived.
   b. Although it was damaged when it arrived.
8. Teresa decided to go to work,
   a. however she had a headache.
   b. although she had a headache.

Reading

1a Read the newspaper article quickly and circle the best title.

    a. Chinese Highways   **b.** Speed Tourists   **c.** Europe's New Destination

(1) For years tourists _____ (1.) to Europe to enjoy its many attractions. From the beaches of the Mediterranean to the castles of Scotland, Europe has something for every kind of vacationer to enjoy. Now travel agents _____ (2.) a new attraction to the list—the German freeway system. For the last three years, travel companies _____ (3.) Chinese tourists to Germany to experience the thrill of driving on its "autobahns." This year more than 120,000 are expected to arrive.

(2) What is it about Germany's autobahns that gets tourists to travel from halfway across the world? The answer is simple—speed. More than 8,000 kilometers (4,971 miles) of German highways have no speed limit—something that is virtually unique in the modern world. Few Europeans realize that Germany's superb roads have an almost mythical reputation in Asia, where highways can be overcrowded, poorly maintained, and full of potholes.

(3) Tour operators _____ (4.) that offering a Mercedes, Audi, or BMW capable of 240 kilometers (149 miles per hour) to tourists is the best way of bringing in much-needed foreign exchange. For the last few years, the Chinese economy _____ (5.)

rapidly and as a result, there are plenty of Chinese travelers wealthy enough to afford the €3,000 ($4,000) charged for a six-day "autobahn tour." The prices they are charging may seem high, but the "speed tourists" claim that the thrill of driving at speeds which would almost certainly lead to prison sentences back at home far outweighs the expense involved.

(4) But this new form of tourism _____ (6.) so popular with the locals. German road safety groups _____ (7.) negatively to the arrival of the Chinese speed tourists. Figures published by the World Health Organization show that more than 600 people die on Germany's roads every year. Even taking into consideration the large population of Germany, this is still a horrifying statistic. But the Chinese drivers are undeterred, pointing out that since they first started coming three years ago, there _____ (8.) no major accidents involving speed tourists.

b Read the article again. Write the questions for these answers on a separate sheet of paper.

    1. three years

    2. 120,000

    3. speed

    4. 8,000

    5. Mercedes, Audi, or BMW

    6. 240

    7. €3,000 ($4,000)

    8. 600

c Find these words or phrases in the article.

    1. two more nouns that mean *tourists*

    _____

    2. three more nouns that mean *roads*

    _____

    3. another expression that means *travel companies*

    _____

    4. an adverb that means *almost*

    _____

    5. an adjective that means *like something from a story or legend*

    _____

    6. an *-ed* adjective that means the opposite of *keep someone from*

    _____

Grammar

2 Complete the article in Exercise 1 using present perfect simple or continuous forms of the verbs in the box.

> add   be   bring   discover
> expand   come   prove   react

3 Answer the questions using the cues and the present perfect simple or continuous. Add other words as necessary.

Ex: *Why are you so red?*
I/lie/sun/all morning
 I've been lying in the sun all morning.

1. Can we go back to the car now?
   no/I/not pay/groceries/yet
   _____

2. Why are the children soaking wet?
   they/swim/the lake
   _____

3. Have you tried that new French restaurant?
   no/yet/be/there
   _____

4. Michael looks tanned.
   yes/he/just/come back/Miami Beach
   _____

5. Why aren't you having any dessert?
   I/be/strict diet/for/last two months
   _____

6. Should I feed the cats?
   no/I/already/do/it
   _____

7. Is Maria still working on that report?
   yes/she/type/lunchtime
   _____

8. You're a good teacher and you seem very experienced.
   yes/teach/karate/more than/ten years
   _____

9. You look exhausted.
   I/wash/the floors/all afternoon
   _____

10. Do you still go to the tennis club?
    no/I/not be/member/2010
    _____

Vocabulary

4 Complete the sentences with adjectives from Exercise 8a on page 70 of the Student Book.

1. **Miranda:** Daniel's behavior made me very angry.
   Miranda feels _____.
   Daniel's behavior was _____.

2. **David:** After listening to her speech, I decided to become a doctor.
   Her speech was _____.
   David felt _____ by the speech.

3. **Mary:** I thought the exhibition was incredibly interesting.
   The exhibition was _____.
   Mary was _____ by the exhibition.

4. **José:** That was the scariest movie I've ever seen. I've never been so scared!
   José was _____ by the movie.
   The movie was _____.

5. **Eloise:** I know the job is difficult, but that hasn't kept me from doing it.
   Eloise doesn't think the job is _____.
   She isn't _____ by the job.

Writing

5 Read the situation. On a separate sheet of paper, complete the email below using the paragraph plan.

Situation: For three months, you have been doing volunteer work as an English teacher to young children. Your job is almost over.

Paragraph 1
where you are/why you are there/how you feel about it

Paragraph 2
what you do in the morning/in the afternoon/in your free time

Paragraph 3
how you feel about the experience/how feel about finishing and coming home

Hi Sara,
I'm having an amazing experience here! I'm . . .

Reading

1a Read the web page. Then write the best heading for each paragraph. Some headings are not used.

   a. Facilities

   b. Reservations

   c. Location

   d. Lapland

   e. History

   f. The Ice Hotel

   g. Construction

b Read the web page again and mark the statements true (*T*) or false (*F*).

   ____ **1.** The Ice Hotel isn't the sort of building people expect to find in a northern country.

   ____ **2.** Local people in Jukkasjärvi don't speak Swedish.

   ____ **3.** It takes two days to build the hotel.

   ____ **4.** The hotel is mainly built of ice.

   ____ **5.** A French artist built the first Ice Hotel.

   ____ **6.** Guests sometimes worry about the cold temperatures.

   ____ **7.** Guests can watch movies.

   ____ **8.** Visitors can hunt reindeer in the daytime.

File   Edit   View   History   Bookmark   help   — X

Unusual Destinations – Number 22

1 People often choose to have vacations in strange places. But few places are stranger than the Ice Hotel in Sweden, which is visited by almost 37,000 people each winter. Built entirely of snow and ice, the hotel is the very opposite of the heavily insulated, centrally heated buildings we normally associate with northern countries. Rather than insulate itself from the cold subzero environment all around it, the hotel embraces the wintry surroundings and makes them into part of its attraction.

2 The Ice Hotel is located in the small village of Jukkasjärvi. Jukkasjärvi lies 200 kilometers (about 120 miles) north of the Arctic Circle in Saamiland (formerly known as Lapland), the northernmost part of Sweden. Before the arrival of the Ice Hotel, there were almost no tourists in this sparsely populated region, where the local people speak Saami, not Swedish, and there is no industry or pollution.

3 The Ice Hotel is not a permanent building; it is rebuilt each winter. Construction of the 5,000 square meter (53,819 sq. ft.) building starts in late October, when special snow cannons shoot tons of snow onto steel sections. After two days, the steel sections are removed, leaving solid snow arches five or six meters wide. Over the following weeks, the sections are reused to make more arches. Huge ice blocks are carved from the frozen river to make walls and pillars. About 30,000 tons of snow and 4,000 tons of ice are used to build the hotel.

4 The story of the Ice Hotel began in the winter of 1989–90. There was an exhibition of ice art in the local village, and a cylinder-shaped igloo made of ice was built for an exhibition by French artist Jannot Derid. Some of the visitors decided to sleep on reindeer skins in the igloo and found it a surprisingly relaxing and stimulating environment. Yngve Bergqvist, the owner of the small local inn, realized that others might want to share this unique experience and the idea for the Ice Hotel was born.

5 Visitors to the Ice Hotel are sometimes nervous about staying in a place where the outside temperature in winter is often minus 40 degrees Centigrade (minus 40 degrees Fahrenheit). But of course, local people have been living in this environment for thousands of years, and conditions inside the Ice Hotel are reasonably comfortable. The temperature is usually around minus four degrees (25 degrees Fahrenheit), and guests are provided with specially made sleeping bags and beds lined with reindeer skins. To keep visitors amused in the evenings, the hotel includes an "ice theater" and an "ice bar." During the day, the hotel company organizes activities such as white water rafting, dogsledding, and fishing. There are also tours of local villages and "safaris" to observe reindeer in their natural habitat.

Grammar

2 Put the words in the correct order to make questions.

Ex: get/when/a/refund/me/can/you/tell/I'll

Can you tell me when I'll get a refund?

1. to/was/who/talking/she

    _____?

2. if/my/do/know/you/this/seat/is

    _____?

3. much/costs/it/can/tell/you/me/how

    _____?

4. they/car/where/the/did/take

    _____?

5. ask/to/the/open/could/I/you/window

    _____?

6. the/how/you/computer/do/turn/off

    _____?

7. correct/are/the/answers/these

    _____?

8. been/how/you/here/long/have/working

    _____?

3 Complete the questions. Then match each question to its answer below.

____ 1. Have you _____ a vacation this year?

____ 2. Where _____ you go?

____ 3. When _____ you go?

____ 4. _____ did you get there?

____ 5. _____ you go on your own?

____ 6. _____ went with you?

____ 7. How _____ did you go for?

____ 8. What _____ it like?

____ 9. _____ it expensive?

____ 10. _____ you going to go again?

a. We flew via Dubai.

b. Fantastic!

c. Three weeks.

d. Yes, probably.

e. To Thailand.

f. Yes, it was.

g. No, I didn't.

h. Yes, I have.

i. My boyfriend.

j. Last January.

4 Use the cues to rewrite the direct questions as indirect questions.

Ex: Where are you from?

Can you _tell me where you are from?_

1. What's your email address?

Can you _____

    _____?

2. Does Paula Rodriguez live here?

Could I _____

    _____?

3. Is this the correct platform for the train to Philadelphia?

Do you _____

    _____?

4. Which seats in the plane have the most legroom?

I'd like to _____

    _____.

5. Who is in charge?

Would you tell _____

    _____?

6. Where exactly does she live?

Can you explain _____

    _____?

7. How much do the tickets cost?

Do you _____

    _____?

8. Is the doctor available now?

Can I _____

    _____?

Communication

1a Read the interviews with a researcher. Match each interview to a statement.

____ **a.** used to live overseas

____ **b.** has seen TV shows about emigrants

____ **c.** definitely isn't interested in living overseas

____ **d.** is planning to live overseas at some point

____ **e.** would like to live overseas but hasn't got any definite plans

b Match each interview to a description of the person being interviewed.

____ **a.** is a student

____ **b.** had problems with travel documents

____ **c.** is in a hurry

____ **d.** is worried about being identified

____ **e.** has family responsibilities

c Read the interviews again. Find words and phrases that mean:

1. thought about (*n.*) _____

2. make someone leave their home (*v.*)

_____

3. depressing (*adj.*) _____

4. giving you a feeling you want to do something (*-ing adj.*) _____

5. this is my true feeling *or* opinion (*phrase*)

_____

6. clearly (*adv.*) _____

7. chances (*n.*) _____

Interview 1

A: Excuse me. Can I ask you some questions about living abroad?

B: Sure.

A: Have you ever considered moving to a foreign country?

B: Not really. I'm very happy with my life as it is! And I have four kids, so it would be hard to uproot them from their schools and friends.

Interview 2

A: Hello. I'm doing some research on emigration. Can I talk to you for a minute?

C: OK, if it's quick. I'm running late.

A: Thanks. Um, have you ever thought about moving to a foreign country?

C: Yes. I love the idea of living somewhere else.

A: Any particular reason?

C: The weather, I suppose. It's so gloomy here in New York in the winter.

A: So you'd prefer to live somewhere hotter?

C: Probably. But I'm not really sure where . . .

Interview 3

A: Excuse me. Can I ask you some questions about living in a foreign country?

D: All right. You don't need my name or anything, do you?

A: No, nothing like that. I'd just like to ask you how you feel about the idea of moving overseas.

D: Oh, do you mean TV shows about people moving to Costa Rica. It always looks tempting.

A: Have you ever thought about doing it yourself?

D: Me? I haven't really thought about it, to be honest.

Interview 4

A: Excuse me. Hello. Could I just take a few minutes of your time? I'm doing some research for a class on people emigrating.

E: Really? I lived in Canada for a year when I was younger.

A: Oh. But obviously you came back . . .

E: Well, I had this Canadian boyfriend. But it didn't really work out. And it was really difficult getting the right visa and everything . . .

Interview 5

A: Hi. Would you mind answering a few questions? It'll only take a minute or two.

F: Sure. No problem.

A: Have you ever considered emigrating?

F: I certainly have. I'd love to do it.

A: Why?

F: Well, the job opportunities, really. I'm in the middle of an engineering degree, and when I finish I'm going to apply for jobs in the Middle East. There are tons of well-paid engineering jobs over there . . .

Vocabulary

2 Match the beginning of each sentence with its end.

_____ **1.** Make sure you've got your passport and tickets before

_____ **2.** See you later tonight. I'm

_____ **3.** I've always dreamed about

_____ **4.** We hate the cold weather here so we're going

_____ **5.** Now that I'm eighteen I think it's time

_____ **6.** She went to Greece and

_____ **7.** His girlfriend didn't even bother to go to the station

a. to emigrate.

b. off to work.

c. to see him off.

d. roamed around the beaches.

e. setting off.

f. living overseas.

g. to leave home.

Grammar

3 Complete the article with the comparative or superlative forms of the words in parentheses. Add other words as necessary.

The Ultimate Thrill

With the latest technological developments, new rollercoaster rides are much _____ (**1.** exciting) ever before. But thrill seekers looking for the ultimate rollercoaster ride are now torn between two monster rides on opposite sides of the world. _____ (**2.** big) is Steel Dragon 2000 in Nagashima Spaland, a theme park in Japan, about 200 miles west of Tokyo. The ride is over one and a half miles long, lasts four minutes and includes a 68 degree drop. At times, riders reach speeds _____ (**3.** great) 95 miles per hour. Costing $55 million, the ride is also _____ (**4.** expensive) ever built.

   Steel Dragon 2000's arch rival is the brand new Kingda Ka ride at Six Flags Great Adventure Park, near Philadelphia, PA, USA. It _____ (**5.** not long) as its Japanese competitor, but what it lacks in size it makes up for in speed and height. With riders traveling at up to 128 miles per hour (206 kilometers per hour) it is by far _____ (**6.** fast) rollercoaster ride on earth.

It is also _____ (**7.** tall), with a maximum height of 456 feet (139 meters). But at less than one minute, the ride is much _____ (**8.** short) the four-minute experience of Steel Dragon 2000.

4 Find and correct the mistakes in each sentence.

1. I think Jeremy's got the most heavy bag.

2. This exercise is more harder than the last one.

3. He was bad hurt in the accident.

4. I'm sorry I arrived so lately; I missed the bus.

5. The Mayback is most expensive car BMW has ever made.

6. They say Rio de Janeiro is always hoter than Buenos Aires.

7. This novel isn't as interesting than his previous one.

8. Antonio lives more far from the school than I do.

9. I'm not as taller as my sister.

10. She speaks Japanese very good.

1 Find and correct the mistake in each sentence.

1. I didn't go with a group; I went as an independence traveler.
2. Experiencing culture shocked can be one of the most difficult parts of living in a foreign country.
3. My sister has always loved traveling—she was bitten by the travel insect as a teenager.
4. I love the unknown; I adore going through uncharted territory.
5. We never go on organized tours, we prefer to wonder around on our own.

2 Complete the article about Bono using past simple, present perfect, or present perfect continuous forms of the verbs in parentheses.

Bono _____ (**1.** be) a rock star for more than the last 25 years. But recently he _____ (**2.** become) famous for something completely different—his work for aid organizations.

Since 2004, Bono _____ (**3.** lead) the fight against poverty in Africa, trying to get more people to understand that continent's terrible problems of famine and disease. For several years now, he _____ (**4.** appear) regularly on TV shows and at international events, attempting to get the world's media to pay attention to this issue. He _____ (**5.** have) meetings with many world leaders and, in 2005, he _____ (**6.** help) organize the Live 8 concerts in London and around the world.

Bono believes his position as an international celebrity _____ (**7.** give) him a unique opportunity to influence young people. He _____ (**8.** visit) Africa several times and these experiences _____ (**9.** clearly influence) his political views. In 2003, Bono _____ (**10.** meet) Nelson Mandela in Cape Town, and in July 2005, he _____ (**11.** speak) to world leaders at the G8 Conference in Scotland, helping to influence their decisions on reducing Africa's debt.

Critics sometimes say that Bono _____ (**12.** only do) this for the last few years to compensate for his group's declining popularity. But with their latest CD high in the charts, this can hardly be the case.

3 Complete the crossword.

Across

3. It's a ____ story, full of twists and turns that keep you hooked.
4. I can't stand cabbage soup, I think it's ____.
7. Babies are often ____ by brightly colored objects.
8. That new horror movie was absolutely ____.
9. It's very ____ when people try to push in front of you at the supermarket check-out line.
10. A lot of people would feel ____ by running a marathon but I take it in stride.

Down

1. I'm a bit ____ about Miriam. Is there something wrong with her?
2. She found the task ____, but she managed to do it in the end.
5. You shouldn't have told the children that scary story, they were ____.
6. Picasso's Guernica was ____ by bombing during the Spanish Civil War.

4 Match the words with their opposites.

____ **1.** clear   **a.** settled
____ **2.** drizzle   **b.** warm
____ **3.** cool   **c.** calm
____ **4.** chilly   **d.** pour
____ **5.** breezy   **e.** sweltering
____ **6.** changeable   **f.** overcast

5 Find and correct the mistakes in the conversation.

> **W:** I'm doing some market research. Could I ask you some questions?
>
> **M:** Sure.
>
> **W:** Where went you for your vacation?
>
> 5 **M:** We went to Florida.
>
> **W:** Who did go on vacation with you?
>
> **M:** My girlfriend.
>
> **W:** Can I ask what is her name?
>
> **M:** Sure. Her name's Lucia.
>
> 10 **W:** Could you tell me what does she for a living?
>
> **M:** Yes. She's a hotel receptionist.
>
> **W:** Do you know how old she is?
>
> **M:** She's 24.
>
> **W:** Can you tell me is she American?
>
> 15 **M:** No. She's Colombian.
>
> **W:** How long she has lived here?
>
> **M:** About six months.
>
> **W:** I'd like to know where did you meet her.
>
> **M:** We met at a party.
>
> 20 **W:** Why did you go to Florida?
>
> **M:** Well, we wanted to see Miami and Key West.
>
> **W:** Would you tell me how long did you stay in Florida?
>
> **M:** We stayed there for three weeks.

6 Circle the correct choice.

1. The neighbors were very noisy, so I had to *move/change house*.

2. When I left for college, my parents came to the station to see me *out/off*.

3. Their daughter lives *overseas/outside,* so they don't see her very often.

4. Over a million Scots *migrated/emigrated* to the USA in the 19th century.

5. The police found a small child roaming *along/around* in the streets.

6. You must be very excited about your trip. When do you *go/set* off?

7. When I was 16, I left *home/house* to join the army.

8. I can't talk now; I'm *off/out* to meet my brother at the bus station.

9. Are you going *over/away* for the long weekend, or are you staying here?

10. She *walked/set* out after they had a terrible argument.

7 Check (✓) the correct phrases to complete each sentence. Sometimes more than one answer is possible.

1. I don't think Barcelona is ____ Malaga.
   - ____ **a.** as sunny as
   - ____ **b.** sunnyer than
   - ____ **c.** sunnier than

2. My new cell phone is ____ my old one.
   - ____ **a.** more good than
   - ____ **b.** a lot better than
   - ____ **c.** many better than

3. He takes life ____ most people his age.
   - ____ **a.** more serious than
   - ____ **b.** more seriously than
   - ____ **c.** just as serious as

4. This model is ____ in the shop.
   - ____ **a.** the less expensive
   - ____ **b.** the most less expensive
   - ____ **c.** the least expensive

5. Los Angeles is usually ____ San Francisco.
   - ____ **a.** not as hot as
   - ____ **b.** hoter than
   - ____ **c.** hotter than

6. Ella arrived ____ the others.
   - ____ **a.** a bit later than
   - ____ **b.** much later than
   - ____ **c.** just as late as

7. Did you drive ____ we did?
   - ____ **a.** more far than
   - ____ **b.** as far as
   - ____ **c.** further than

8. Bill Gates is ____ in the US.
   - ____ **a.** the richest man
   - ____ **b.** the man richest
   - ____ **c.** the most rich man

UNIT 7
Indulging yourself

LESSON 1

Communication

1a Read the conversation. Answer the questions on a separate sheet of paper.

1. How many speakers are there?
2. What are they trying to decide?
3. What do they decide to do in the end?

Carla: I haven't eaten since lunch and I'm starving. Do either of you feel like going out to pick up some food?

Ben: Great idea, Carla. I'm ravenous.

Seiko: Me too. Could you get something for me, too?

Carla: What would you like?

Seiko: Um. I'm not sure. A burger, I guess.

Carla: OK. What about you, Ben?

Ben: I'm not too excited about burgers. How about fried chicken or something?

Seiko: Oh, that's disgusting. It's so greasy.

Carla: Actually, I was thinking about a pizza. There's that new pizza place near the post office. It's called Pizza Delight, or something like that. How does that sound?

Seiko: Yummy. I love pizza.

Ben: Yuck. I'm sick of pizzas. I've had them twice this week already.

Carla: I thought you were on a diet, Ben.

Seiko: Yeah. He's on the pizza diet!

Ben: Very funny, Seiko. And I suppose burgers are super healthy.

Seiko: Well, I bet they're not as fattening as pizzas. Anyway, I was going to have a vegetarian burger.

Ben: A vegetarian burger? They're completely tasteless. Like eating cardboard!

Carla: Look. There's no point in arguing. We need to agree on something.

Ben: What about a hot dog?

Carla: Oh, no. I had one of those a couple of days ago and it gave me a stomachache.

Seiko: I know. What about Chinese?

Ben: Good idea. There's a Chinese restaurant on Arnold Street. It's just around the corner from the supermarket. They do that delicious Peking Duck . . .

Carla: Yes. And they have those wonderful king prawns. Great. Chinese it is!

---

b Read the conversation again and check the correct column.

	Carla	Ben	Seiko
1. wants to eat a burger			
2. likes fried chicken			
3. suggests going to a pizza place			
4. loves pizza			
5. is supposed to be on a diet			
6. thinks burgers aren't as fattening as pizzas			
7. doesn't like vegetarian burgers			
8. loves king prawns			

c Find these adjectives and phrases in the conversation. Write them in the correct column.

---

greasy　　　starving　　　delicious
yummy　　　tasteless　　　ravenous
not too excited about　　　disgusting
to be sick of something

Feeling very hungry	Positive opinion	Negative opinion

Grammar

2 Circle the correct words to complete the brochure.

Riverside Technical College
Student Facilities

Here are just _____ (1.) the facilities we provide for our students. We hope you'll agree that we have something to offer everyone!

Computer and Internet Center

You're always connected at Riverside! We have _____ (2.) computers available, all with free wifi access to the Internet. There are _____ (3.) wireless printers too—so you can print out your essays with ease. And if you need _____ (4.) advice, we have full-time computer technicians available 24/7.

Student Café and Bar

_____ (5.) students enjoy their lunch here. We have a huge range of delicious and healthy snacks, including salads and sandwiches. We're open until midnight, so why not invite _____ (6.) friends and spend the evening with us? Or just drop in for _____ (7.) cup of coffee and a slice of our homemade cake.

College Sports Center

Why not improve your health with _____ (8.) exercise? Riverside has an extensive range of sports facilities. We have state of the art exercise machines and a fabulous heated swimming pool. Our students spend _____ (9.) their free time here. There are _____ (10.) colleges in the country which can rival our sports-club facilities, and it's all free for students!

1. a. few   c. a few of
   b. some
2. a. much   c. any
   b. many
3. a. lots of   c. much
   b. any
4. a. an   c. some
   b. many
5. a. Few   c. Much
   b. A lot of
6. a. a few   c. few
   b. a little
7. a. a   c. little
   b. a piece of
8. a. many   c. a little
   b. little
9. a. many   c. a lot
   b. a great deal of
10. a. a few   c. few
    b. little

3 Check (✓) the correct sentences in each pair. Sometimes both sentences are correct.

1. _____ a. I eat two eggs every morning.
   _____ b. She got egg all down the front of her dress.
2. _____ a. He bought me some chocolates for my birthday.
   _____ b. She's diabetic, so she can't eat chocolate.
3. _____ a. I need some legal advice.
   _____ b. The doctor gave her three advices.
4. _____ a. My new car has excellent equipments.
   _____ b. Will you bring the camping equipment?
5. _____ a. Pedro's knowledge of computers is impressive.
   _____ b. Knowledge are very important in the modern world.
6. _____ a. I often feel nostalgic for the old times.
   _____ b. There never seems to be enough time.

Vocabulary

4 Complete the sentences with words from the box. Some words are not used.

> sauce pan   scramble   bake   fry
> frying pan   bitter   grill   boil

1. During the summer, we often have friends over and _____ some burgers.
2. Donna just put some water on to _____, so we can have some tea soon.
3. This coffee is too _____. Can I have some sugar and milk for it?
4. To make a creamy sauce, first melt some butter in a deep _____, and then mix in a little cream and lemon juice.
5. Jason makes a great stir-fry. He mixes lots of different vegetables in a _____ with a little oil and some meat.
6. For breakfast, I usually _____ some eggs and eat them with toast.

Reading

1a Read the article below quickly and circle the best title.

    a. Impressionist Paintings at Sotheby's

    b. The Story of Sotheby's

    c. The World's Greatest Auction House

b Read the article again. Match the names with the information.

___ **1.**	Sotheby's	**a.**	John Sotheby's rival
___ **2.**	Samuel Baker	**b.**	chairman of Sotheby's
___ **3.**	James Christie	**c.**	the most famous auction house
___ **4.**	Peter Wilson	**d.**	an American businessman
___ **5.**	Parke-Bernet	**e.**	John Sotheby's uncle
___ **6.**	Alfred Taubman	**f.**	a New York auction house

c Fill in the blanks in the article using the correct forms of the verbs in parentheses.

d Find the words or phrases in the article that mean:

    1. worth a lot of money (*adj.*) _____

    2. copy someone's example (*phrase*) _____

    3. effect, impression, or influence (*n.*) _____

    4. best or highest quality examples of works of art (*n.*) _____

    5. time when the economy is bad (*n.*) _____

    6. completely (*adj.*) _____

(1) There is little doubt that Sotheby's is the oldest and most famous auction house in the world. It has been going for more than two and a half centuries, and has sold many of the most famous and valuable treasures and works of art ever created. Many would say that the international art market as it exists today _____ (**1.** create) by Sotheby's. The idea of enormously valuable works of art being sold at public auction is something we take for granted, but in fact, it is a relatively new phenomenon. So how did it all start?

(2) It all began back in 1744 when a book dealer called Samuel Baker opened a small London book store in the Strand. After his death in 1778, the business _____ (**2.** take over) by his nephew, John Sotheby. Sotheby had a great rival, James Christie, who _____ (**3.** start) Christie's auction house in 1776. Buying and selling things at auction was made fashionable by James Christie, but John Sotheby was quick to follow his lead. In 1793, he auctioned famous French diplomat

Talleyrand's library and in 1823 he _____ (**4.** score) a public-relations triumph by auctioning Napoleon's collection of books from St. Helena.

(3) Sotheby's business grew throughout the 19th century, but it was only in the middle of the 20th century that Sotheby's began to make a huge impact internationally. In 1958, its chairman, Peter Wilson, _____ (**5.** organize) the first ever public auction of Impressionist masterpieces by Cezanne, Renoir, and Van Gogh. Before that time, extremely valuable works such as these, _____ (**6.** sell)

privately or through dealers. Wilson turned the whole auction into a fashionable event. He sent invitations to movie stars and politicians and held the auction in the evening. Journalists from the leading newspapers _____ (**7.** invite). Not surprisingly, the auction got a huge amount of publicity and the prices set new records.

(4) With its growing reputation in London, Sotheby's decided to expand into the American market and bought New York auction house Parke-Bernet. But things began to go wrong during the recession of the 1970s, and the company got into financial difficulties. Eventually, in 1983, Sotheby's _____ (**8.** buy) by American businessman, Alfred Taubman. Based in Detroit, Taubman transformed Sotheby's into a wholly American company. It was certainly a long way from the little bookshop in the Strand.

Vocabulary

2 One word in each sentence is incorrect. Find and correct the word.

1. It's a good idea to keep the refund when you buy expensive things.
2. If we buy ten of these, can we get a bargain of 10%?
3. Auctions are fun, but I do get nervous when people start haggling for something I want.
4. I want to buy a new computer but I can't worth it yet.
5. I love buying things in street markets—it's great fun bidding with the market traders.
6. They're moving next year, so they're not sure if it's afford buying a new sofa.

Grammar

3 Rewrite the sentences in *italics* in the factsheet on a separate sheet of paper. Use <u>only</u> passive forms.

Money Factsheet 8

1. ***How does the mint make coins?***
   Long sheets of metal arrive at the mint.
2. *Somebody feeds the metal strips into a cutting machine.*
3. *The cutting machine cuts the metal into round shapes called "blanks."*
4. *After the machine has cut them out, somebody heats the blanks in a furnace.*
5. *Somebody washes the blanks while somebody is heating them.*
   The hot blanks go into a pressing machine.
6. *The machine stamps each coin with a pattern on both sides.*
7. *Somebody cools the coins and a special machine counts them.*
8. *Somebody distributes the coins to the banks.*

4 Rewrite each sentence with the words given.

Ex: Peter published the report last year.
The report <u>*was published last year*</u>.

1. The doctor has given Alison a new prescription.
   Alison _____.
2. You shouldn't open the present until your birthday.
   The present _____.
3. The police are investigating the crime.
   The crime _____.
4. They are going to open the hotel in November.
   The hotel _____.
5. We will drive the children to the party.
   The children _____.
6. You can see my house from the top of the hill.
   My house _____.
7. Somebody was watching them.
   They _____.
8. They haven't released that DVD yet.
   That DVD _____.
9. Somebody might have seen the burglar.
   The burglar _____.
10. They didn't take anything.
    Nothing _____.

Writing

5 On a separate sheet of paper, rewrite this informal letter as a formal letter of complaint. Use the information on page 144 of the Student Book to help you.

Dear James O'Brien,

I'm writing to tell you about a cell phone I bought in your store the other day.

When I got home, it didn't work. I was really shocked because it cost $250!

Please send me another phone or give me a refund immediately.

I'd love to get a reply soon.

Love,
Mandy Smith

Communication

1a Read five people's comments about animals. Match each speaker with an animal from the box. Some animals are not mentioned.

> snake   cats   spider   tropical fish
> mouse   dog   horse   goldfish

1. _____   4. _____

2. _____   5. _____

3. _____

b Match each statement with an animal from Exercise 1a. Write the animal on the line.

1. is always hungry _____
2. lives in a big field _____
3. need a lot of care and attention _____
4. loves going for walks _____
5. doesn't jump any more _____
6. provide companionship _____
7. moves very slowly _____
8. costs a lot of money to maintain _____

c Find the words from the box in the speakers' comments. Put them in the correct columns below.

> dart   crawl   sinuous   gentle   stable
> trot   tank   kennel   playful

Ways animals move (verbs)	Places animals live (nouns)	Animal characteristics (adjectives)

Speaker 1

Well, I'm not really sure you'd call them pets. I mean, obviously you don't have to take them to the vet or for walks. But they do require quite a lot of care and attention. I spend a lot of time cleaning out the pond and repairing the water filters. It's a nightmare in the fall with all the fallen leaves. And in winter, you have to make sure the surface doesn't get covered in ice. But watching them darting around gives me a lot of pleasure.

Speaker 2

We've had him for about four years now. He's got a kennel in the backyard. His name's Wolfie. David bought him for the children. Everyone knows retrievers are great with kids—so gentle and playful. He has beautiful, blond fur and he loves being cuddled. Of course, he adores being taken for walks—which is a great excuse for us to get some exercise as well. The only downside is he eats a lot of food. And whatever we give him, he always seems to be starving.

Speaker 3

Some people think keeping a reptile is a little bit weird, but you'd be surprised at how popular it is. I know tons of people that do it. I got Sarah from a friend and I wasn't too sure about her at first. It's kind of a hassle because you have to have a big tank and keep it at a certain temperature. And when she sheds her skin it's a little disgusting. But I think she's beautiful—the way she moves is so slow and sinuous. I love letting her crawl up my arms and around my neck.

Speaker 4

When I was younger, I used to take her out jumping and stuff, but I hurt my back a few years ago so now we just go for walks—or a gentle trot if I'm feeling energetic. We have a big field behind the house, so she's got plenty of room, and there's a small stable for the winter. Big animals are always pretty expensive to care for, but I think it's worth it. I mean, I get plenty of exercise, and I feel we have a really strong bond. I certainly wouldn't let anyone else ride her.

Speaker 5

I never had any children, but I think in some ways they're better than children. A lot less trouble! I've got two at the moment, Tiddles and Spark. Tiddles is just a kitten, really. Now that I'm retired, I don't really get out much so they're ideal for me, and they're much easier to take care of than dogs. They're pretty independent, but they give me a lot of companionship. I talk to them all the time, which is a little weird I know, but at least I don't get lonely.

Grammar

2 Complete the sentences with nouns from box A and verbs from box B. Use *have/get something done*.

A	
car	blood pressure
hair	house eyes

B		
check	test	do
paint	wash	

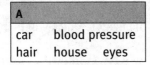

1. Mrs. Alderson

_____

every month.

2. Daniel

_____

once a week.

3. The Smiths

_____

every five years.

4. Liz _____

once every six

months.

5. Mr. Grant _____

when he goes to the doctor.

3 Rewrite the sentences using the words in parentheses.

Ex: He needs to finish that project soon. (done)

He needs to get that project done soon.

1. Somebody left the bag behind. (got)

_____

2. The maid washes Linda's clothes. (has)

_____

3. They forward my mail to me. (I)

_____

4. Will somebody cut your hair this week? (get)

_____

5. How often do they clean your windows? (you)

_____

6. I should finish my homework by six o'clock. (done)

_____

Vocabulary

4 Complete the crossword with animal words.

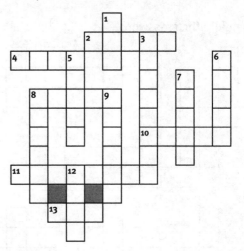

Across

2. they can be very sharp
4. it lives in the sea
8. to take the bull by the ____
10. symbol of the USA
11. they keep birds warm
13. if you see this above the water it could be a shark

Down

1. planes and birds do this
3. cats have very long ones
5. straight from the ____'s mouth
6. the biggest animal
7. birds couldn't fly without them
8. toenails for a horse
9. lots of people are afraid of this insect
12. it's at the back of a horse or dog

1 Complete the crossword.

Across

5. Heat the milk in a small ____.
7. You have to ____ the mixture quickly until it becomes stiff.
9. I don't eat meat. I'm a ____.
13. The soup isn't ____ enough, add a little more.
14. This vegetable contains a lot of vitamins.
15. It's a fruit which we often serve with cream.

Down

1. Don't cook my steak for very long, I like it ____.
2. They say ____ are very good for you.
3. You haven't cooked this, it's completely ____.
4. Coffee without sugar has this taste.
6. I don't put sugar in tea or coffee—I hate ____ drinks.
8. Do you prefer to ____ eggs or fry them?
10. Chili dogs are very ____.
11. I like to ____ a little parmesan cheese on top of my pasta.
12. Would you like a ____ of cake?

2 Complete the sentences with words from the box. Some words are not used.

> spending   extra-large   excessive
> spoiled   far-fetched   overpriced
> luxury   extravagant

1. My car isn't a _____; it's a necessity.
2. You're renting a five-star hotel for your wedding? How _____!
3. Some people say there is life on Mars, but the idea seems _____ to me.
4. After we moved, we went on a _____ spree and bought lots of new furniture.
5. Don't buy anything from that store—all their goods are very _____.
6. I think it's greedy to order _____ portions in restaurants.

3 Find and correct eight mistakes in the sentences.

1. Our store stocks luggages from all over the world.
2. There are few places as beautiful as Cancún.
3. There isn't many traffic around here on Sundays.
4. May I have little sugar in my coffee, please?
5. I'd like to have a lots of money.
6. They're not very busy, they only have a few work this week.
7. They don't have much money, but they're happy.
8. Would you like a spaghetti, or do you prefer rice?
9. You can invite few of your friends to the party if you like.
10. The college offers much foreign language classes.

4 Read the web page and complete the sentences below with passive forms.

Thank you
for booking with

Your booking reference is HJ980L

We have charged $450 to your credit card. For your security, we use 128 KB protection software for all credit card payments.

We are sending your itinerary by email. We will send your tickets by first class mail.

Please note the following:

- You must bring your passport to check-in two hours before departure.
- You cannot change the date and time of your flights.
- You can select seats on the website.
- GoAway Travel does not allow smoking on any of its flights.
- You may purchase meals on the plane.
- The price includes transfers from the airport.

Please see our FAQs if you have any more questions.

Ex: $450 *has been charged to your credit card.*

1. 128 KB protection software _____ _____.

2. Your itinerary _____ _____.

3. Your tickets _____ _____.

4. Your passport _____ _____.

5. The date and time of your flights _____ _____.

6. Seats _____ _____.

7. Smoking _____ _____.

8. Meals _____ _____.

5 Complete the sentences using words from the box.

> bargain   haggling   refund
> bidding   discount   receipt

1. I only paid $10 for this DVD—I got a _____!

2. We love visiting the local markets and _____ for things.

3. I'm afraid you cannot return the goods if you do not have a _____.

4. Don't interrupt him; he's _____ for something on an Internet auction site.

5. We are offering a 20% _____ to any customers who buy more than five CDs.

6. Due to the cancelation of tonight's performance, we are offering a full _____ to all ticket holders.

6 Complete each sentence.

1. I _____ the heater checked last month so it should be fine now.

2. She never received her new credit card—it must have _____ lost in the mail.

3. I'm sorry about spilling wine on your jacket. I'll have it _____ for you.

4. Tell the boss that Jamie will _____ the report done by four o'clock.

5. Have you gotten the broken chair _____?

6. I like to have my hair _____ by Silvia. She's the best stylist in the salon.

7. I'm going to get my photo _____; I need it for the job application.

8. It blocks the light so we are _____ that big tree removed.

7a Cross out the incorrect word in each group.

1. A bull has: hooves   horns   fin   tail
2. A cat has: whiskers   beak   paws   claws
3. An eagle has: feathers   wings   paws   beak
4. A bear has: hooves   fur   paws   claws

b Complete the sentences.

1. I'm worried that I won't get this job, but I need to take the _____ by the _____ and apply anyway.

2. Don't ask Grandma to read the instructions; she's as _____ as a _____.

LESSON 1

Reading

1a Read the biography quickly. Write the best heading for each paragraph. Some headings are not used.

  a. The Fight for Freedom

  b. Independence

  c. Studying in London

  d. Introduction

  e. Gandhi's Legacy

  f. Gandhi's Early Life

  g. Life in Prison

  h. Philososphy

b Read the biography again. Mark the statements true (*T*) or false (*F*).

  _____ **1.** Gandhi was president of India.

  _____ **2.** Gandhi worked in South Africa.

  _____ **3.** South Africa used to be part of the British empire.

  _____ **4.** Local people were sometimes treated badly in the colonies.

  _____ **5.** The British were never able to put Gandhi in prison.

  _____ **6.** Some elements of Satyagraha come from Hinduism.

  _____ **7.** Gandhi wanted India to be mainly Hindu.

  _____ **8.** A religious extremist killed Gandhi.

c Make notes to complete this time-line of Gandhi's life.

1869	born in Porbandar,
1893	
1915	
1947	
1948	

Leading by Example

① _____

Gandhi is one of history's great leaders. But unlike other leaders, he never led an army, he was never a president or prime minister, and he never used force or violence to impose his leadership on people. His principle of leadership was simple—he led by example. He believed that the best way to influence events was through peaceful protest rather than by violent revolution or bloodshed.

② _____

Mohandas Karamchand Gandhi was born on October 2, 1869, in Porbandar, in western India. He was sent to England to study law and was offered a job in South Africa after he qualified in 1893. At that time, both India and South Africa were colonies of Britain. Working as a lawyer, Gandhi soon began to experience the prejudice that local people suffered under the colonial regime.

③ _____

Gandhi returned to India in 1915, determined to fight against colonialism and injustice. He realized that Indians would never be able to build a fair society until they were independent from the British. He joined the Indian nationalist movement and began to fight for Indian independence. The British regarded Gandhi as a troublemaker, and he was arrested many times. Gandhi was prepared to be sent to prison for his beliefs. Altogether, he spent more than seven years behind bars.

④ _____

Most independence movements in history have depended on violent revolution to achieve their aims. Gandhi was sure that the same effect could be achieved through non-violent protest and a policy of civil disobedience. He developed a philosophy known as "Satyagraha" that was partly based on the teachings of Hinduism. According to Satyagraha, the best way to change society was through peaceful means. Through his own behavior, Gandhi provided an example of this philosophy in action.

⑤ _____

After more than 30 years of struggle, India eventually achieved independence in 1947. Gandhi's policy of peaceful protests, strikes, trade boycotts, and civil disobedience had worked. Gandhi wanted India to be a single country that included all races and religions, but his wish was not granted. The Indian sub-continent was split into two states—the mainly Hindu India and the largely Muslim Pakistan.

⑥ _____

Gandhi's belief in religious freedom was to cost him his life. On January 30, 1948, he was assassinated by a young Hindu fanatic, Nathuram Godse. But his legacy was to last long after his death. Gandhi's philosophy of peaceful protest and civil disobedience has been an inspiration to numerous people around the world. By his own actions, he showed that the best leaders are those who lead by example, rather than by force.

Grammar

2 Circle the sentence that has the same meaning as the sentence in *italics*.

1. *It's time you went to bed.*
   a. You should be in bed by now.
   b. You are already in bed.

2. *I'd rather take the bus.*
   a. There is no other way to get there.
   b. I prefer buses to the subway.

3. *We'd better take the earlier flight.*
   a. We prefer early flights.
   b. The later flight might not arrive in time.

4. *Would you rather I replied by email?*
   a. I prefer to send emails.
   b. Do you want me to send an email?

5. *It's high time you looked for a job.*
   a. You've been looking, but you haven't found the perfect job yet.
   b. You are unemployed and haven't looked for a job.

6. *I'd rather she didn't come.*
   a. I don't want her to come.
   b. She doesn't want to come.

7. *You'd better take the car.*
   a. It's a good idea to drive.
   b. You prefer driving.

3 Rewrite the sentences using the words in parentheses.

1. I really think you should move to a bigger apartment. (cheap)
   _____

2. You should take an umbrella. (better)
   _____

3. I prefer going to the movie theater. (rather)
   _____

4. John needs to get a better computer. (about)
   _____

5. Do you want me to bring my camera? (would)
   _____

6. I would prefer her not to smoke. (didn't)
   _____

7. I don't like working on the weekend. (rather)
   _____

8. I think it's safer if you have the salad. (you'd)
   _____

Vocabulary

4 Complete the crossword with words to describe personality.

Across

1. Carol's really high ____; she needs expensive presents all the time!

5. I've got strong ideas about everything; I suppose I'm pretty ____.

6. He doesn't have any secrets. He's very ____ and honest.

10. Actors love an audience because they like to be the center of ____.

11. Tania's ____; she likes meeting new people and she talks to everybody.

12. We always laugh when Jake tells a story because he's so ____.

13. My boss is very single-____; he never gets distracted.

Down

1. My girlfriend tricks people into doing what she wants; she's very ____.

2. Liz never makes a fuss or complains; she's very ____-going.

3. ____ people always do what they want and refuse to listen to advice.

4. To be a good lawyer, you need to be ____-to-earth and realistic.

7. I wish I could be more ____, but I tend to let other people take the lead.

8. Juanita goes out to clubs every night, she's a real ____ animal.

9. You shouldn't be such a ____; try to be more assertive and independent.

Communication

1a Read the conversation. Answer the questions on a separate piece of paper.

1. Where are they?
2. What is Amanda's job?
3. What are Steven's goals?

Amanda:	Come on Steven, keep going.
Steven:	This is exhausting . . .
Amanda:	One more repetition. You can do it . . . Great. Good work. Let's take a short break now.
Steven:	Phew! Good idea!
Amanda:	You're doing really well.
Steven:	I still find it very difficult.
Amanda:	Well, you can't expect to get in shape in just a month.
Steven:	(1.) *Actually, it's been six weeks.*
Amanda:	Six weeks then. You know it usually takes about three months to get in shape. After all, you haven't done any real exercise for more than five years, so you have some catching up to do.
Steven:	Hmm. It seems like a really long time.
Amanda:	Think positive. We're almost halfway there.
Steven:	(2.) *How long before I start to feel healthier?*
Amanda:	That depends. Have you cut out sweet snacks?
Steven:	Uh, sort of. But I'm still eating desserts. I just feel so hungry all the time.
Amanda:	(3.) *How about trying fruit instead of a dessert?*
Steven:	OK. (4.) *I will give it a try.*
Amanda:	(5.) *If you cut down on the amount of sugar you eat, you're sure to feel better.* How about your energy level? Are you still feeling tired in the afternoons?
Steven:	No, that's definitely improved. I don't really feel as tired as I used to.
Amanda:	That's great.
Steven:	Oh, have you prepared that nutrition sheet for me?
Amanda:	Sorry. (6.) *I'm afraid I forgot.* I'll do it next week. So, are you ready to move on to the next machine?
Steven:	Gosh. You trainers are such slave drivers!

---

b Read the conversation again and complete each statement.

1. Steven has been training for _____ weeks.
2. He hasn't done any real exercise for _____ years.
3. Steven thinks three months is a _____ long time.
4. He is _____ eating desserts.
5. He _____ hungry all the time.
6. Amanda asks Steven about his _____ level.
7. Steven used to feel _____ in the afternoons.
8. Amanda hasn't prepared the _____ sheet for Steven yet.

Vocabulary

c Match the phrases from the conversation in *italics* with the verbs in the box.

____ ask	____ admit	____ promise
_1_ remind	____ explain	____ suggest

---

d Find six examples of direct speech from the conversation in Exercise 1a. Write them in reported speech, using reporting verbs from the box.

---

admit	promise	suggest
~~warn~~	explain	ask

Ex: Amanda _warned Steven (that) he couldn't expect to get into shape in just a month._

1. Amanda _____
_____

2. Steven _____
_____

3. Amanda _____
_____

4. Steven _____
_____

5. Amanda _____
_____

2 Complete the sentences with *absolutely* (non-gradable adjectives) or *really* (gradable adjectives).

1. I always feel _____ hungry after swimming.

2. I often feel _____ tired at the end of the day.

3. Terry was _____ devastated when the factory closed down.

4. Suzanne was _____ exhausted after the race.

5. Poor Joe! He's _____ upset about his exam results.

6. What's there to eat? I'm _____ starving!

Grammar

3 Circle the correct words to complete the sentences.

1. When we were young our parents ___ not to talk to strangers.
   a. told   b. told to us   c. told us

2. James asked me what ___ for my birthday.
   a. I wanted   b. did I want   c. wanted me

3. My girlfriend asked me ___ go to the party with her.
   a. will I   b. if I would   c. that I would

4. He said ___ already bought the tickets.
   a. me he had   b. he had   c. to me he had

5. The sales assistant suggested ___ a new MP3 player.
   a. buying   b. to buy   c. me buying

6. The criminal promised ___ out of trouble.
   a. to stay   b. staying   c. he will stay

7. The police officer warned me not ___ so fast in the future.
   a. driving   b. to driving   c. to drive

8. Michael asked us ___ the movie last Wednesday.
   a. did we enjoy   c. if we enjoy
   b. if we had enjoyed

9. She asked me whether ___ a school uniform when I was in elementary school.
   a. I must wear   c. did I have to wear
   b. I had to wear

10. Davina asked me ___ been the day before.
    a. where I had   c. where was I
    b. where had I

4 Change the direct speech to reported speech using the verbs from the box. Use each verb once.

admit	decide	promise	explain
warn	~~remind~~	suggest	

Ex: David Don't forget to lock the back door.

David reminded me to lock the back door.

1. **My brother** Why don't we go out for a meal?

_____

_____

2. **John** I can't come because I have to work that evening.

_____

_____

3. **The children** We'll never do it again.

_____

_____

4. **The lifeguard** Swimming there can be very dangerous.

_____

_____

5. **Maria** I haven't done my homework.

_____

_____

6. **Customer** I'll take the smaller model.

_____

_____

Reading

1a Read the newspaper article and match the people with their descriptions.

____ 1. Piers Sharma   a. took a Math GCSE at the age of five.

____ 2. Mike Ryde   b. is a college principal.

____ 3. Arran Fernandez   c. is taking a GCSE next year.

____ 4. Francesca   d. is six years old.

____ 5. Frederick   e. is waiting for his exam results.

Who's the smart aleck?

Is it wise for children aged six and seven to be taking advanced level exams, asks Zoe Brennan

Like many youngsters across the UK, Piers Sharma will be waiting for the mailman with trepidation next month when exam results come out. At just seven years old, he is not the average student, however.

"It was a little bit hard, and a little bit easy," he says of the exam in computer skills. "The hard part was the video conferencing; the applications part was easy."

Does he expect to pass? Sharma sounds momentarily stressed. "I did really well in the practical hands-on section, I got an A+," he says. "In the written exam, I might have got a C+ or B+."

The test that Sharma took is standard in the UK, and is called the GCSE. The GSCE is a secondary school qualification, and is the equivalent of a high school diploma exam. Most students do their GCSEs at the age of fifteen or sixteen, but Sharma is one of a growing number of pupils taking exams extraordinarily early. This year, he is one of an entire class of nine children—four seven-year-olds and five six-year-olds—who, in May, took a GCSE in information and communication technology (ICT) at the private Ryde College in Hertfordshire, England.

The class takes a year to complete. Mike Ryde, principal of the college, confirmed that three of the children were five years old when they embarked on their GCSE studies, having "graduated" from the college's baby and toddler computer class, where learning starts at eighteen months. At the age of three or four, the children attend "primer" lessons. Then Ryde judges when they are ready to take the exam.

"The most we've ever had before has been one or two children of this age doing a GCSE," says Ryde. The fact that we've got nine students this year shows that a lot of six and seven-year-olds would be capable of doing this. It is no coincidence that they all started in classes so early."

The youngest ever to have taken a GCSE at Ryde was Arran Fernandez, who was five when he took the math GCSE in 2001. Ryde's own daughter, Francesca, who is seven years old, will take the ICT GCSE next year and his son, Frederick, who is six, is on the primer course. "The wonderful thing is that studying at a level designed for a fifteen-year-old has a knock-on effect," he says. "Francesca is topping the class at school."

"We also have children taking English and Math exams really early, but the younger children seem to gravitate towards ICT," he says. "They love working with computers."

Many educators and parents are horrified and argue that six is too young to burden a child with exams. Ryde, however, believes that early GCSEs should be introduced everywhere, claiming that such a system would reduce the stress on youngsters later on.

"At present, you see children taking more than ten GCSEs at once when they are 16," he says. "That's a tremendous pressure. Why not give them the opportunity to take one or two of these exams a year? It seems to me that most children are ready to do a GCSE by the age of 11. We should not dumb down the system to the lowest common denominator—education is all about opportunity."

b Read the article again and correct the factual mistakes in the statements.

1. Exam results are coming out later this month.

2. Piers Sharma got an A+ in the exam.

3. There are five students in Piers' class at school.

4. The college has a math class for babies.

5. Mike Ryde's son is top of the class at school.

6. The parents decide when children are ready to take an exam.

7. Mike says the older children love working with computers.

8. Mike thinks few children could take a GCSE at the age of eleven.

c Match these words and phrases from the article with their meanings.

____ 1. momentarily   a. when two things are the same for no reason

____ 2. extraordinarily   b. surprisingly

____ 3. embarked   c. lower the standard

____ 4. coincidence   d. causes other things to happen

____ 5. domino effect   e. shocked, frightened

____ 6. gravitate   f. for a very short period of time

____ 7. horrified   g. are attracted towards

____ 8. dumb down   h. began

Grammar

2 Complete the picture labels using *hard* and *hardly*. Add other words as necessary.

1. It was very disappointing. _Hardly anyone_ came to my barbecue.

2. Roberto tries really _____ but I don't think he'll ever succeed.

3. I can't help you. I've got _____ any money myself.

4. I'm not surprised Jane's work is so bad, she _____ comes to the class.

5. I'm afraid there's _____ left to eat in the fridge.

6. We looked _____ but we couldn't see where our friend was.

3 Complete the sentences with the words and phrases from the box.

hard (x2)	hardly anything
hardly (x2)	hardly anywhere
hardly ever (x2)	hardly anyone (x2)

1. You've _____ touched your food!
2. This is a treat; we _____ go to restaurants these days.
3. Although Sam studied _____, he wasn't able to pass the test.
4. By ten o'clock, there was _____ left in the club.
5. Our teacher _____ gives us homework.
6. Monica pushed _____ but she couldn't open the door.
7. There's _____ to park in Manhattan.
8. I didn't spend much; I bought _____.
9. I've _____ seen Isabel since she got married.
10. _____ on my street owns a car.

4 Read the conversation and circle the correct choices.

Nobuko: Did you see that item about students on the news? It said that nowadays more than half of them take a year off between school and college. They call it a "gap year."

Jake: What do they do?

Nobuko: They usually go traveling. I *am thinking/think* (**1**.) it's a really good idea.

Jake: I disagree. As far as I'm *concerned/ concerning* (**2**.), it's a waste of time.

Nobuko: Well, I *trust/believe* (**3**.) it can be a very useful experience.

Jake: Why do you think that?

Nobuko: Well, *for/because* (**4**.) several reasons. For example it gets them away from their parents and makes them more independent.

Jake: Getting a job and earning your own money is what makes people independent, *of/in* (**5**.) my opinion.

Nobuko: That's true. But, students taking time off often get jobs while they are traveling *for/because* (**6**.) they need money to live on.

Jake: I thought their parents usually paid for everything.

Nobuko: Perhaps some of them do, but I don't think that's a very good idea. I mean, if the parents pay for everything, *so/then* (**7**.) their children are never going to become independent.

1 Match the beginning of each sentence with its end.

_____ **1.** If this product doesn't sell, the company will definitely

_____ **2.** Deborah's delighted—the book she wrote has become a

_____ **3.** People don't watch cowboy films any more; I think they've

_____ **4.** I think you'll have to pull it down and start again; this work really isn't

_____ **5.** We've never done this before, but we're willing to

_____ **6.** After failing his driver's test four times, Jim has decided to

a. up to snuff.

b. best-seller.

c. give up.

d. go under.

e. give it a try.

f. had their day.

2 Complete each sentence with one word.

1. It's getting late; I think it's _____ we left.

2. Would you _____ take the bus or the train?

3. Your bedroom's filthy; it's _____ time you tidied up.

4. Look at those dark clouds, you'd _____ take an umbrella.

5. I'm a little tired; I _____ rather not go out this evening.

6. Don't you think it's about time you _____ your mother—you can use my cell phone.

7. She's looking very sick; you _____ better call a doctor.

8. _____ you rather pay me now or wait until next week?

9. You'd better _____ interrupt him right now, he's with a client.

10. I'd rather _____ poor and happy than rich and unhappy.

3 Circle the correct choice.

1. My cousin doesn't have unrealistic ideas; he's very down to _ground/earth_.

2. I'm pretty _headstrong/proactive_—I don't pay attention to what other people think.

3. Isabel loves parties; she's very _outgoing/easy-going_.

4. My boss can be very _opinionated/manipulative,_ so I don't really trust him.

5. You must invite Mi-hyun to the party; she's very _high maintenance/witty_ and she'll make us all laugh.

6. Everyone takes advantage of David, but then, he's a complete _doormat/doorway_.

7. We're looking for a new marketing manager who will be _proactive/open_ about developing the business.

8. Like all actors, he loves to be the _heart/center_ of attention.

9. Don't be so _selfish/single-minded_; leave some of the chocolate for us.

10. She never listens to reasonable arguments; she's very _opinionated/single-minded_.

4 In six sentences the adjective in _italics_ is incorrect. Find and correct the mistakes.

Ex: Alex was very ~~devastated~~ _upset_ when he heard the news.

1. My apartment is in a great location but it's absolutely _small_.

2. Miranda loves cleaning, her kitchen is very _spotless_.

3. The children were really _exhausted_ after their skiing lesson.

4. I'm really _hungry_. What's in the fridge?

5. The guided tour of the castle was absolutely _interesting_.

6. It's absolutely _vital_ that you take out the correct insurance.

7. Roberto was very _ecstatic_ about his pay raise.

8. New York can be absolutely _cold_ in January.

5 Match the direct speech in a–j with the sentence beginnings below. Then complete the sentences with reported speech.

___ a. Don't touch these plates, they're very hot.

___ b. Where's your passport?

___ c. I'm afraid the doctor's sick today, so he can't see you.

___ d. Don't forget to be at the airport two hours before your departure.

___ e. Do all the exercises on page 65 of the Workbook.

___ f. I'll pay back the loan within six months.

___ g. Are you feeling all right, honey?

___ h. Why don't we go to the movies on Friday evening?

___ i. I stole the money.

___ j. I think I'll have the spaghetti Bolognese.

1. The receptionist explained _____
_____ .

2. Our teacher told us _____
_____ .

3. My best friend suggested _____
_____ .

4. The waitress warned us _____
_____ .

5. The criminal admitted _____
_____ .

6. The immigration officer asked me _____
_____ .

7. My mother asked me _____
_____ .

8. The customer decided _____
_____ .

9. The travel agent reminded us _____
_____ .

10. Elizabeth promised the bank manager _____
_____ .

6 Circle the correct word or phrase to complete the sentence.

1. If you ____, you can just see the north star above the horizon.
   a. hardly look   **b.** look hard   **c.** hard look

2. Hardly ____ came to the show.
   a. nobody   **b.** none   **c.** anyone

3. She ____, but she couldn't reach the top shelf.
   a. tried hard   **b.** hardly tried   **c.** hard tried

4. John made one last effort and hit the hammer as ____ as he could.
   a. hardly   **b.** hard   **c.** very hardly

5. I thought last night's homework was ____.
   a. so hardly   **b.** a lot hard   **c.** very hard

6. Since he got married, we ____ our son.
   a. hardly never see   **c.** hardly are seeing
   b. hardly ever see

7. ____ in this store is in our price range.
   a. Hardly nothing   **c.** Anything hardly
   b. Hardly anything

8. I can't go out this week, I've got ____ left in my bank account.
   a. hardly no money   **c.** hardly any money
   b. hardly money

9. After the accident I ____ my arm.
   a. could hardly move   **c.** couldn't hardly move
   b. could move hardly

10. Running the marathon was ____ work.
    a. really hard   **c.** really hardly
    b. hard of

Reading

1a Read the stories quickly. Write the best headline for each story. Some headlines are not used.

- **a.** Fatal Coffee
- **b.** The Unlucky Car Thief
- **c.** Imprisoned in a Garage
- **d.** Nightclub Accident
- **e.** Don't Ask the Jury
- **f.** Cruise Control

Compensation Culture or Legal Legends?

1. _____

In December 2002, Joseph Grazinski bought a brand-new motorhome. He was thrilled because it had cruise control—a switch on the steering wheel that controls the accelerator and maintains the vehicle's speed at a constant rate. A few days after buying the motorhome, he decided to take it on a trip to Yellowstone National Park. Having entered the freeway, he set the cruise control at 65 mph and decided to step into the back of the motorhome to make himself a cup of coffee. Within seconds, the motorhome had veered off the road, slid down a hillside, and turned upside down. Mr. Grazinski broke an arm and a leg and suffered cuts to his head.

Mr. Grazinski sued the manufacturers because it did not say in the owner's manual that it was dangerous to leave the steering wheel while driving, even if the cruise control was switched on. The court awarded him $175,000 and a brand-new motorhome.

2. _____

In April 1998, Kara Walton of Claymont, Delaware wanted to get into the Black Cat nightclub but she didn't want to pay the $3.50 cover charge. So, she decided to sneak into the club by climbing through the window of the ladies bathroom. Unfortunately, while struggling to get through the window, she fell to the floor and knocked out her two front teeth.

Ms. Walton sued the owner of the Black Cat nightclub and was awarded $12,000 compensation plus dental expenses.

3. _____

For ten years, Terrence Dickson of Bristol, Pennsylvania, had had a successful career as a burglar who specialized in robbing people's houses while they were on vacation. In October 2004, he was about to leave a house he had just robbed when he got stuck in the garage. After entering the garage from the house, he realized the door could not be opened from the inside. Because the owners were on vacation, he was trapped in the garage for another eight days. During this time, he lived on the supply of dog food and some cans of cola that the owners kept at the back of the garage.

Mr. Dickson sued the homeowner's insurance company, claiming that he had been the victim of kidnapping, starvation, and mental torture. The jury awarded him $500,000 compensation.

b Find these words and phrases in the stories and write them in the correct columns in the chart.

cruise control	suffered
compensation	speed
owner's manual	broke
knocked out	court
accelerator	jury
starvation	mph
awarded	fell
expenses	

Vehicles	Injuries or Harm	Legal

c Read the stories again, and write questions for the answers.

Ex: It maintains the vehicle's speed.
 What is the cruise control?

1. To make himself a cup of coffee.

2. A broken arm and leg and cuts to the head.

3. To avoid paying the cover charge.

4. $12,000.

5. For ten years.

6. Because the owners were on vacation.

7. A supply of dog food and some cans of cola.

Grammar

2 Underline three examples of sentences containing sequencing devices in the stories in Exercise 2.

3 Read the sentences. Circle the action that happened (or started) first, a or b.
1. Having taken two aspirin, I began to feel a little sick.
   a. taking two aspirin   **b.** began to feel sick
2. Before going to bed, I have a glass of milk.
   a. going to bed   **b.** have a glass of milk
3. After leaving home, he got a job in a circus.
   a. leaving home   **b.** got a job in a circus
4. On hearing the news, I rushed out to tell my girlfriend.
   a. hearing the news   **b.** rushed out
5. Having crashed his car, Gerry had to come by taxi.
   a. coming by taxi   **b.** crashed his car
6. While waiting for the train, I noticed a small child crying on the platform.
   a. waiting for the train   **b.** noticed a child

4 Rewrite the sentences using the words in parentheses.
Ex: Karl took the test then he went out to celebrate. (taken)
 Having taken the test, Karl went out to celebrate.

1. Dave told his best friend before he announced the news to his co-workers. (having)

2. He got up and went into the village to get some food. (after)

3. They went to bed after they had watched the midnight movie. (going)

4. Surinda was watching TV when she heard a strange sound. (while)

5. Before we went to the computer store we read lots of consumer reports. (reading)

6. Jackie had to get a taxi because she missed the bus. (having)

7. The kids usually do their homework and then watch TV for an hour. (doing)

Vocabulary

5 Complete each sentence with the correct form of a word from the box.

appeal	convict	premium	sue
arson	fraud	sentence	

1. The judge _____ the man to three years in prison.
2. There was a fire at the factory last week. Police think it was _____.
3. I fell down the steps at work, so I _____ the company and got compensation.
4. You shouldn't use someone else's credit card. That's _____.
5. The _____ on our car insurance seems to get higher every year.
6. The criminal decided to _____ the court's ruling.
7. He was _____ of armed robbery.

Grammar

1 Match the questions with their answers below.

___ 1. Why didn't she pass the test?
___ 2. Why did she marry him?
___ 3. Why did she get an A+ on the test?
___ 4. Why did she divorce him?
___ 5. Why didn't she come to work?
___ 6. Why did she do that job?
___ 7. Why didn't she say hello to me?
___ 8. Why was she waving?

a. She must have fallen in love.

b. She might have been sick.

c. She can't have loved him any more.

d. She can't have seen you.

e. She might have needed the money.

f. She can't have studied hard enough.

g. She must have seen you.

h. She must have done lots of work.

2 Rewrite the sentences in *italics* using *must*, *might*, or *can't have*.

1. The plants look very healthy. *Somebody definitely watered them.*

   _____

2. Emma isn't here. *Perhaps she didn't receive the invitation.*

   _____

3. *I'm sure he didn't go out.* I saw the light on in his bedroom.

   _____

4. Their apartment is empty. *I'm certain they have left already.*

   _____

5. *I'm sure they haven't left the country.* They don't have passports.

   _____

6. Peter isn't answering his cell phone. *Maybe he forgot to take it with him.*

   _____

7. *Maria's probably passed the exam.* She studied very hard.

   _____

8. Where's your umbrella? *I'm absolutely sure you forgot to bring it.*

   _____

3 Complete the article with *must*, *might*, or *can't have*.

The Mystery of Tutankhamen's Tomb

The discovery of Tutankhamen's tomb is all thanks to one man, Howard Carter. If it hadn't been for Carter's endless curiosity and persistence, the incredible tomb _____ (1.) been lost forever. Carter was working in the Valley of the Kings, in Egypt, when he noticed an ancient pile of trash near the entrance of the tomb of Rameses VI. Carter realized that the trash _____ (2.) been there for a reason, and he asked his men to dig into it. Three meters below the original surface, they found a stone step carved into the side of the valley. From its depth and position, he knew that this step _____ (3.) been at least three thousand years old. It turned out to be the first of many steps that led down to the fabulous tomb of Tutankhamen.

It took Carter many months to fully excavate the tomb. But then the archaeologist was left with just as many questions as answers. Who exactly was Tutankhamen and how had he died? From the size of the body, he knew that Tutankhamen was only a boy, he _____ (4.) been more than eighteen or nineteen when he died. But what killed him? He _____ (5.) been murdered by a jealous relative or he _____ (6.) died from disease. From the inscriptions in the tomb, Carter knew that Tutankhamen _____ (7.) come to the throne at the age of about eight or nine. Since he died young, he _____ (8.) been on the throne for more than about ten years. Yet his tomb was filled with fabulous treasures, worthy of a great king.

Communication

4a Read the transcript of a radio interview. Circle the best answers.

1. There will be _____ guests on the show.
   - **a.** none
   - **b.** one
   - **c.** more than one

2. The radio show is probably designed for _____.
   - **a.** lawyers
   - **b.** 16- to 18-year-olds
   - **c.** young children

3. Emily says the majority of lawyers work _____.
   - **a.** in court
   - **b.** for criminals
   - **c.** in offices

4. Divorce is part of _____.
   - **a.** civil law
   - **b.** criminal law
   - **c.** court

5. Emily thinks the most important quality of a defense attorney is _____.
   - **a.** self-confidence
   - **b.** communication
   - **c.** a good memory

b Read the interview again and complete the quotes.

1. "There's a factsheet that you can _____ from our website."

2. "Emily will help us _____ some of the mysteries of the legal profession."

3. Criminal attorneys "present the case for either the prosecution or _____ the accused."

4. "Only a small _____ of lawyers actually work in court."

5. "What sort of _____ qualities do you think a good attorney needs?"

6. "You've got to _____ you know what you're doing."

c Complete the sentences with words and phrases from Exercise 5b.

1. I am writing this letter _____ the board of directors.

2. You're very tanned. You _____ you've been somewhere sunny.

3. I'm going to _____ some MP3 songs from the Internet.

4. This isn't the _____ behavior I expect from someone like you.

5. Can you help me _____ these cables, they are all jumbled up.

6. You should try to have a large _____ of vegetables in your diet.

Zack: Hello, everyone, and welcome once again to Job Spotlight. On today's show, we'll be looking at job opportunities in the legal profession. From your letters and emails, I know this is a career that a lot of you are considering, so we've put together some support. There's a factsheet that you can download from our website. My first guest in the studio today is top lawyer Emily Johnson. Emily will help us unravel some of the mysteries of the legal profession.

Emily: Hello.

Zack: Welcome to the show, Emily. Now, you're a defense attorney, aren't you?

Emily: Yes, a criminal defense attorney.

Zack: Can you tell us exactly what a defense attorney does?

Emily: I'll do my best. Actually, I think most people are familiar with criminal attorneys from TV and movies. We're the people who stand up in court and present the case either for the prosecution or on behalf of the accused, that's the person accused of a crime.

Zack: Don't all lawyers do that?

Emily: Not really. Only a small proportion of lawyers actually work in court. Most lawyers work in offices—helping people buy houses, make their wills, get divorces—that kind of thing.

Zack: You said you were a criminal attorney. Does that mean you work for criminals?

Emily: No, not exactly. It means I work in criminal law rather than civil law.

Zack: So, what's the difference?

Emily: Well, criminal law has to do with actual crimes—murder, arson, robbery, and so on. Civil law isn't about crimes at all; it's the law that governs things like contracts, inheritance, business, things like that.

Zack: So, you wouldn't be able to help me if I wanted to get a divorce.

Emily: I'm afraid not. Well, not unless divorce suddenly became a crime!

Zack: Yeah, right. Now, for our listeners who are thinking about becoming criminal defense attorneys, what sort of qualities do you think a good attorney needs?

Emily: I think the main one is self-confidence. You've got to look like you know what you're doing. And communication is very important, especially in court.

Zack: I suppose a good understanding of human nature comes in handy.

Emily: Yes, and a good memory helps, too.

Zack: OK. Let's talk about the training you need to do . . .

Reading

1a Read the book review quickly. Which statement is correct? _____

    a. It summarizes the complete plot and characters of *The Hound of the Baskervilles*.

    b. It describes Conan Doyle's career using *The Hound of the Baskervilles* as an example.

    c. It gives the background to *The Hound of the Baskervilles* and introduces the story.

b Read the book review again. Mark the statements true (*T*) or false (*F*).

    _____ **1.** *The Hound of the Baskervilles* was originally a series of magazine stories.

    _____ **2.** People believe that a hound has killed Sir Charles Baskerville.

    _____ **3.** Sir Charles was Henry Baskerville's uncle.

    _____ **4.** Henry Baskerville comes to see Sherlock Holmes.

    _____ **5.** Dr. Mortimer is a friend of Sherlock Holmes.

    _____ **6.** Dr. Mortimer has some shocking new evidence about the mystery.

    _____ **7.** Sherlock Holmes believes in scientific explanations.

    _____ **8.** Holmes and Watson immediately solve the mystery.

c Find these words in the review. From their context, decide if they are verbs, nouns, or adjectives. Then match them with their definitions.

    _____ **1.** cliff-hanger   _____ **5.** heir

    _____ **2.** curse   _____ **6.** consult

    _____ **3.** beast   _____ **7.** inquest

    _____ **4.** estate   _____ **8.** rational

    a. (*n.*) an animal (especially a wild or dangerous animal)

    b. (*n.*) a legal process that examines the causes of a person's death

    c. (*v.*) ask for advice from an expert

    d. (*n.*) magic to make sure that something terrible will happen

    e. (*n.*) a large area of land with a house that belongs to one person or family

    f. (*adj.*) scientific and logical

    g. (*n.*) an exciting development in a plot that makes the reader want to know more

    h. (*n.*) somebody who inherits land or money when a relative dies

Sherlock Holmes and *The Hound of the Baskervilles*

① *The Hound of the Baskervilles* is one of the most famous and admired detective stories ever written. Published in 1901 and 1902, it originally appeared in nine monthly installments in *The Strand* magazine. Like Dickens's serialized novels of the same era, each installment ended with a suspenseful "cliff-hanger" that kept author Sir Arthur Conan Doyle's audience clamoring for more.

② In the story, the old and noble Baskerville family is threatened by a curse: "A great, black beast, shaped like an enormous wild dog or hound, yet larger than any hound that has ever been seen" terrorizes and kills any family member who comes to live at the Baskerville estate. As the story opens, the hound seems to have claimed its latest victim, Sir Charles Baskerville. Sir Charles's nephew, Henry, the new heir to the estate, is about to take up residence the next day. A friend of the family, Dr. Mortimer, comes to consult the famous Sherlock Holmes in his rooms at 221b Baker Street, though he admits he doesn't know if the case is more suitable "for a detective or a priest." The first installment of the novel originally ended as Dr. Mortimer explains:

③ *". . .One false statement was made by Barrymore at the inquest. He said that there were no traces upon the ground round the body. He did not observe any. But I did—a short distance away, but fresh and clear."*

    "Footprints?"

    "Yes, footprints."

    "A man's or a woman's?"

    Dr. Mortimer looked strangely at us for an instant, and his voice sank almost to a whisper as he answered: "Mr. Holmes, they were the footprints of a gigantic hound!"

④ Into this atmosphere of ancient secrets, deadly curses, and supernatural beasts comes the supremely rational Sherlock Holmes—a man described by his friend Watson as "the most perfect reasoning and observing machine the world has ever seen." Piece by piece, Holmes and Watson solve the mystery and find the culprit. In the end, they reassure the characters in the novel (as well as Conan Doyle's Victorian readers), that behind the threat of a supernatural "hound of hell" is a perfectly scientific explanation.

Grammar

2 Match statements 1 and 2 with their correct explanations a and b.

1. ____ 1. We stayed in the only hotel in the town that had a sea view.

   ____ 2. We stayed in the only hotel in the town, which had a sea view.

   a. There were several hotels, but only one had a view of the sea.

   b. There was only one hotel in the town.

2. ____ 1. My sister, who lives in Paris, just had a baby.

   ____ 2. My sister who lives in Paris just had a baby.

   a. I have several sisters, and one of them lives in Paris.

   b. I only have one sister.

3. ____ 1. All the students, who can speak French, were invited to the party.

   ____ 2. All the students who can speak French were invited to the party.

   a. All of the students were invited to the party.

   b. Some of the students were invited to the party.

4. ____ 1. The theater, which is across from the station, is going to become a nightclub.

   ____ 2. The theater that is across from the station is going to become a nightclub.

   a. There is only one theater in our town.

   b. There is more than one theater in our town.

3 Complete the sentences with relative clauses using the information from the box. Add commas and relative pronouns if necessary.

> The hospital is very old.　~~She is Spanish.~~
> He was elected last year.　He was Scottish.
> I'm living in that house.
> I saw that movie yesterday.
> We met the girl on vacation.
> Her boyfriend lives in Athens.
> We stayed in the hotel last summer.

Ex: John's sister-in-law, _who is Spanish_, is training to be an opera singer.

1. Miranda's boyfriend _____ is a doctor.

2. The house _____ is over a hundred years old.

3. Arthur Conan Doyle _____ was born in 1859.

4. The president _____ has introduced a new tax.

5. Our local hospital _____ is about to be closed down.

6. The girl _____ is coming to stay next weekend.

7. Spielberg's new movie _____ was fantastic.

8. The hotel _____ had a heated swimming pool.

Writing

4 Write a short story based on these pictures. Use the guidelines on page 146 of the Student Book to help you.

1   Use the clues to complete the crossword.

Across

1. The ____ stole my purse while I was dancing.

4. The murderer was given a ____ of 30 years in prison.

6. After the car crash, we had to ____ the other driver for compensation.

7. That wasn't an accidental fire; it was ____ .

9. Rather than send her to jail, the judge ordered her to complete six months of community ____ .

10. The pictures from the store's cameras helped to ____ the shoplifter in court.

11. Credit card ____ is one of the fastest-growing crimes.

Down

2. The police found him because he left his ____ on the weapon.

3. Although she has been convicted, her lawyer is going to make an ____ to a higher court.

5. In a courtroom, the ____ has the most power.

8. My car insurance ____ went up by 20% this year.

10. We filed an insurance ____ after our luggage was stolen.

11. He's going to ____ a lawsuit against the boys who stole from him.

2   Circle the correct answer.

1. Before *leaving/left* the meeting, she handed me her business card.

2. Having *seeing/seen* the movie myself, I wouldn't recommend it.

3. *At/On* arriving at the airport, the tourist group was met by the travel agent.

4. *After/Before* taking the pills, I felt a lot better—they were very effective.

5. Having opened the door, she *runs/ran* into the garden.

6. While *lived/living* in New York, Kirsten made many new friends.

3   Read the article. Complete the sentences below with the correct forms of *must*, *might*, or *can't have*.

Last night $50,000 was stolen from the safe of Western United Bank. None of the doors or locks was broken, so the police think somebody working in the bank stole the money. There were no fingerprints on the safe door, but the police found a cigarette butt on the floor near the safe. Nobody is allowed to smoke in the bank. Only three members of the staff have keys to the safe: Mr. Briggs, the manager, Jennifer, the assistant manager, and Darren, the chief cashier. Mr. Briggs was at home with his wife all last night. His wife confirms this. Jennifer says she was at home, but she lives alone. Darren says he was at home. He lives with his parents. His mother says he was at home all night, except when he went outside to take the dog for a walk at midnight.

1. The money _____ been stolen by the staff because no doors or locks were broken.

2. It _____ been Mr. Briggs, Jennifer, or Darren because they are the only ones with keys to the safe.

3. The thief _____ been a smoker because there was a cigarette butt on the floor.

4. It _____ been Mr. Briggs because he was at home with his wife all night.

5. Jennifer _____ stolen the money because she can't prove where she was.

6. Darren _____ stolen the money when he went out for a walk at midnight.

4 Complete the sentences with compound adjectives. The first letter of each adjective is given.

1. This cake is delicious. Is it h_____?
2. I never buy second-hand things. I like everything to be b_____.
3. Yes, sir. A first class ticket to Seoul— o_____ or return?
4. I'm afraid we only have p_____ jobs available right now.
5. You can tell from her writing that she's l_____.
6. It was a l_____ decision to come here because we didn't know our vacation dates until last week.
7. I find filling in all this paperwork incredibly t_____.
8. She's really determined and s_____ about getting what she wants.
9. Car insurance is much cheaper for m_____ people than for youngsters.
10. I really wouldn't trust that s_____ friend of yours; she's really dishonest.

5 Six sentences contain grammar and punctuation mistakes. Find and correct the mistakes.

1. My brother that works in Cardiff is an opera singer.
2. Jen of who I told you about last week is getting married.
3. The house we saw last weekend is worth over $1 million.
4. The children didn't pass the test had to take it again.
5. Our car that we bought last year has been stolen from our garage.
6. The movie was on TV last night was absolutely fascinating.
7. Pilar, who guided us around the town, is a real expert on Argentinian history.
8. My co-worker, which showed us how to use the computer has been promoted, to the Los Angeles office.

6 Combine each sentence pair to make one sentence. Use defining and non-defining relative clauses.

Ex: The house has been sold. It is the house where I used to play as a child.
   The house where I used to play as a child
   has been sold.

1. It belonged to an old lady. The old lady died.
   _____

2. When I was young, the old lady allowed me to play in her garden. The old lady used to be a schoolteacher.
   _____

3. The garden had lots of lemon trees. The garden was huge.
   _____

4. I used to pick the lemons from the trees. The trees grew there.
   _____

5. The old lady used the lemons to make lemonade. I had picked the lemons.
   _____

7 Read the newspaper headlines. Mark the statements below true (*T*) or false (*F*).

Manchester United bids for top Chinese player

NBC to axe top comedy show

Senators clash over immigration

French Actress quits Hollywood

President backs strikers

CHILDREN RESCUED FROM HOTEL BLAZE

_____ 1. Manchester United has hired a Chinese soccer player.
_____ 2. NBC will cancel a popular comedy show.
_____ 3. Government officials disagree about immigration.
_____ 4. A French actress has left Hollywood.
_____ 5. The president wants the strikers to go back to work.
_____ 6. Firefighters have rescued some children from a hotel fire.

LESSON 1

Communication

1a Read the radio show transcript and choose the best summary.

   a. The transcript is a book review.

   b. The transcript is an interview with a writer.

   c. The transcript is about a famous French hypnotist.

b Use the transcript to complete the notes on Franz Mesmer's life. Write one word or number in each gap.

1734	• born in _____ (1.)
1766	• _____ (2.) a doctor from _____ (3.) University • started using _____ (4.) on sick patients
1777	• moved to _____ (5.). • became famous treating French _____ (6.), he even treated the _____ (7.). • he cured people but he also _____ (8.) them.
1785	• he was _____ (9.) to go back to Germany.
_____ (10.)	• he died

c Match words and phrases 1–8 with the things they refer to a–d.

   _____ **1.** quite unique

   _____ **2.** a kind of magic

   _____ **3.** a great showman

   _____ **4.** a recently discovered phenomenon

   _____ **5.** were treated by Mesmer

   _____ **6.** surprisingly effective

   _____ **7.** like theatrical displays

   _____ **8.** gullible

   a. Franz Anton Mesmer

   b. Mesmer's treatments of patients

   c. French aristocrats

   d. magnetism

I: This week's biography choice is *Mesmer—The Original Hypnotist*. It is the story of Franz Anton Mesmer, the 18th-century scientist who is often regarded as the founder of hypnotism. With me in the studio is the book's author, Alexander Bond. Alexander, can I start by asking you what attracted you to this character?

B: Yes. Well, I've always been interested in hypnotists and I wanted to find out how hypnotism first started, so obviously that led me to Franz Mesmer.

I: Now, Mesmer is quite unique, isn't he?

B: Yes. He's one of the very few people whose name has become an English verb.

I: As in "to be mesmerized by something" . . .

B: Exactly. And that shows just how influential and important he was.

I: He was French, wasn't he?

B: Actually, he was born in Germany, in 1734. And he studied medicine in Austria—at the University of Vienna, in fact.

I: So how did he first became famous?

B: Well, after he graduated a doctor in 1766, he started doing experiments with magnets. Magnetism was a recently discovered phenomenon but it wasn't understood very well. People saw metal objects flying towards each other, and it seemed to be a kind of magic. Anyway, Mesmer started applying magnets to his sick patients . . .

I: To sick people?

B: Yes. In fact, it was surprisingly effective. Lots of his patients got better, and Mesmer soon became the best-known doctor in Vienna. But the other doctors resented his success and forced him to move to Paris in 1777.

I: And that's where he became really famous?

B: Yes. Paris was pretty much the center of European culture at the time, and the French were fascinated by Mesmer and his magnetic cures. Many members of the French aristocracy were treated by him. Even King Louis XVI became one of his patients. But then, Mesmer was a great showman, his treatments were more like theatrical displays, so as well as curing people, he entertained them.

I: But how did it work?

B: Well, we think that what he was really doing was hypnotizing people. From detailed descriptions written at the time, it seems he probably used the power of hypnotism to convince his patients they were feeling better.

I: He must have made a lot of money from those gullible French aristocrats!

B: Yes, he made a fortune. But his success didn't last for long. He failed to cure some influential members of French society and in 1785, he was forced to go back to Germany, where he lived until 1815.

Vocabulary

2 Find and correct the unnecessary or incorrect word in each sentence.

1. Are you in favor that the law against smoking in restaurants?
2. He's convenienced that the government is lying to us.
3. The police suspect of the murderer knew the victim.
4. I'm against give money to street people.

Grammar

3 Circle the correct words to complete the sentences.

1. They've got an oven that cleans ____.
   - **a.** himself
   - **b.** itself
   - **c.** them
2. Our teacher told ____ to do Exercise 3.
   - **a.** ourselves
   - **b.** we
   - **c.** us
3. It's very important to concentrate ____ you are driving.
   - **a.** while
   - **b.** you while
   - **c.** yourselves
4. I hurt ____ when I was lifting a heavy suitcase.
   - **a.** myself
   - **b.** me
   - **c.** my
5. Emma sat down and relaxed ____ 20 minutes.
   - **a.** her for
   - **b.** herself for
   - **c.** for
6. The children really enjoyed ____ on the rollercoaster.
   - **a.** themselves
   - **b.** itself
   - **c.** themself
7. We couldn't afford builders so we decided to build the house ____.
   - **a.** myself
   - **b.** another
   - **c.** ourselves
8. When he went on vacation, David took his computer with ____.
   - **a.** itself
   - **b.** himself
   - **c.** him

4 Rewrite the sentences on a separate sheet of paper using reflexive pronouns.

Ex: Janna looked at her reflection in the mirror.
Janna looked at herself in the mirror.

1. Darren cut his hand while he was gardening.
   _____
2. I made the cake without anyone's help.
   _____
3. We've made all the arrangements; nobody helped us.
   _____
4. My central heating turns on automatically if the temperature drops.
   _____
5. The Bensons often send packages to their home address when they are abroad.
   _____
6. Did you paint this picture on your own?
   _____
7. Isabel doesn't work for anybody else; she's self-employed.
   _____

5 Put the words in the correct order to make questions.

1. about/do/you/strong/feelings/have/pollution/any
   _____ ?
2. poverty/feel/how/about/do/you
   _____ ?
3. the/for/are/death/penalty/you/or/against
   _____ ?
4. on/what/fast/food/are/views/your
   _____ ?
5. think/divorce/of/what/do/you
   _____ ?

Reading

1a Read the article quickly. Circle the best summary.

    a. Artificial smells haven't lived up to expectations.

    b. Artificial smells have huge potential for business.

    c. Banks hope artificial smells will increase their profits.

b Read the article again. Mark the statements true (*T*) or false (*F*).

    ____ **1.** Dale Air has produced an artificial "smell of money" for Barclays Bank.

    ____ **2.** The bank is having problems with its air conditioning systems.

    ____ **3.** It is difficult to isolate the real smell of money.

    ____ **4.** Shoppers are aware of the effect smells have on their spending.

    ____ **5.** The smell of coconuts seems to encourage people to book vacations.

    ____ **6.** Cafés often put coffee machines near the entrance.

    ____ **7.** The human sense of smell is highly developed.

    ____ **8.** Most of the scientific problems of producing artificial smells have now been solved.

c Find the words and phrases in the article that mean:

    1. a compound adjective to describe bread that has just been made _____

    2. an adjective meaning the opposite of *pessimistic* _____

    3. a phrasal verb that means *to collect or attract something* _____

    4. a compound noun that describes a machine used to store money in a store _____

    5. an adverb we use when something is done in a clever and almost invisible way _____

    6. a scientific phrase that describes the parts of the body we smell things with _____

    7. an adjective made from the verb *to evoke* _____

    8. a verb that means *to control something and use it for your own benefit* _____

The Smell of Money

For many years, large supermarkets have been encouraging us to spend money by pumping the smell of freshly-baked bread into their stores. Now Dale Air, a leading firm of aroma consultants, has been approached by Barclay's Bank to develop suitable artificial smells for their banks. Researchers have suggested that surrounding customers with the "smell of money" will encourage them to feel relaxed and optimistic and give them added confidence in the bank's security and professionalism.

But before a smell can be manufactured and introduced into banks' air conditioning systems, it must be identified and chemically analyzed, and this has proved to be difficult. The problem is that bills and coins tend to pick up the smell of their surroundings. So cash that has been sitting in a cash register at a fish store will smell like fish, and bills used to pay for meals in restaurants tend to smell like food.

It may be a challenge, but aroma experts have little doubt that the use of artificial smells can be an effective form of subconscious advertising. Lunn Poly, a British travel company, introduced the smell of coconuts into its travel agencies and saw a big increase in spending by vacation goers. Many cafés now have electric dispensers that release the smell of freshly roasted coffee near their entrances, subtly encouraging customers to come in and have a drink or snack. Even the prestigious car maker Rolls-Royce has been spraying the inside of its cars to enhance the smell of the leather seats.

"The sense of smell is probably the most basic and primitive of all human senses," explains researcher Jim O'Riordan. "There is a direct pathway from the olfactory organs in the nose to the brain." It is certainly true that most people find certain smells incredibly evocative, stirring memories and feelings in a way that few other stimulants can rival. It is a phenomenon marketing consultants have long recognized, but until recently have been unable to harness. "We've made great progress but the technology of odor production is still in its infancy," says O'Riordan. "Who knows where it will take us."

Vocabulary

2 Label items 1–4 with words from the box. Some words are not used.

> hype   marketing   advertisement
> brands   classified ad   target market
> slogan

"You deserve the best"

1. _____

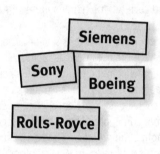

2. _____

For Sale
2003 Toyota Corolla
40,000 miles
Excellent condition.
$3,000
Tel (555) 643-2101

3. _____

Married women living in the
United States between the
ages of 30 and 45 with annual
incomes in excess of $35,000.

4. _____

Grammar

3 Circle the correct choice.

1. Did your co-workers *refuse/suggest* working on the weekends?
2. The boss suggested *join/joining* her for lunch.
3. Let me know when you've finished *writing/to write* the report.
4. He encouraged *her to get/to get her* a new job.
5. Could you *promise/imagine* living without a cell phone?
6. Sheila should practice *speaking/to speak* Spanish before she goes to Venezuela.
7. Will you *miss/agree* playing basketball on Saturdays?
8. Did you persuade her *coming/to come*?

4 Match the beginning of sentences 1 and 2 with their ends a and b.

1. ____ 1. I stopped watching TV
   ____ 2. I stopped to watch TV
   a. and answered the phone.
   b. because there was a fascinating documentary on.

2. ____ 1. I regret to say
   ____ 2. I regret saying
   a. you were lazy; it was very rude of me.
   b. that you have not been selected for the team.

3. ____ 1. I remember locking the door before
   ____ 2. Remember to lock the door before
   a. you go home.
   b. I left.

4. ____ 1. Hilary tried closing the door but
   ____ 2. Hilary tried to close the door but
   a. there was still a cold draft in the room.
   b. it was jammed and she couldn't do it.

Writing

5 Write an essay using one of these titles.
- Pollution is the most serious threat facing the modern world.
- The death penalty should be used for all convicted murderers.
- Fast food is dangerous to people's health and should be banned completely.

Look at the guidelines in Exercise 9b on page 121 of the Student Book to help you.

Reading

Mind Control—is it real?

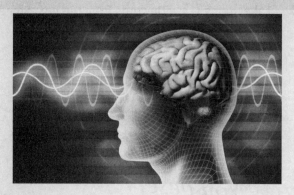

1a Read the article quickly. Write the best heading for each paragraph. Some headings are not used.

  a. Subconscious Suggestion

  b. The Future

  c. Advertising

  d. Fiction or Reality?

  e. Pavlov

  f. New Drugs

  g. Conditioning and Indoctrination

b Read the article again and write questions for the answers.

  1. _____ ?

  Memories of a failed romance.

  2. _____ ?

  Changes in brain chemistry.

  3. _____ ?

  More than forty.

  4. _____ ?

  Through subtle suggestion and manipulation.

  5. _____ ?

  By endlessly repeating tasks and sequences.

  6. _____ ?

  Which parts of the brain control individual movements.

c Find words or phrases in the article that mean:

  1. something invented *or* not true (*n.*) (paragraph 1) _____

  2. chemicals made from several different ingredients (*n.*) (paragraph 2) _____

  3. people who study the brain (*n.*) (paragraph 2) _____

  4. take away *or* remove (*v.*) (paragraph 2) _____

  5. surprised *or* impressed (*-ed adj.*) (paragraph 3) _____

  6. getting people to do what you want by secretly tricking them (*n.*) (paragraph 3) _____

  7. instructions given to you by a superior (*n.*) (paragraph 4) _____

  8. do a task (*phrasal v.*) (paragraph 4) _____

  9. distorted information given to people by a government or organization to influence them (*n.*) (paragraph 4) _____

① _____

After the release of *Eternal Sunshine of the Spotless Mind,* the subject of mind control was once again in the news. In the movie, Joel has bad memories of a failed romance removed from his mind by the sinister Lacuna organization. Of course, the movie was only fiction. But could such a thing happen in real life?

② _____

Scientists point to the recent development of several drugs which appear to influence the brain. Known as memory-management drugs, these new compounds can cause changes in brain chemistry, and seem to directly influence the part of the brain that stores and processes past experiences. Neuroscientists hope to make products that can improve memory skills and even erase negative thoughts. The American Food and Drug Administration (FDA) is testing more than 40 such products.

③ _____

Drugs are not the only way the mind can be controlled. Viewers of a TV series on mind control featuring British illusionist Derren Brown have been amazed at how he can put ideas into people's minds through subtle suggestion and manipulation. Similar effects are achieved by hypnotists, although they always claim they are only harnessing the mind's own hidden desires and wishes. Some people even claim that advertisements include invisible triggers that stimulate the subconscious to make us want particular products.

④ _____

More traditional forms of mind control are well-known. For centuries, armies have been training soldiers to obey orders without thinking using a method now known as Pavlovian conditioning. It was named after Russian psychologist Ivan Pavlov. By endlessly repeating tasks and sequences and by employing simple tactics of punishment and reward, people can be persuaded to carry out instructions without question. On a larger scale, the technique of indoctrination can be employed. Through the use of education and propaganda, dictators and governments throughout history have convinced people of things that are untrue.

⑤ _____

The future holds even more worrying possibilities. Research has shown us exactly which parts of the brain control individual movements. Once we have learned how to stimulate these areas, we will be able to make people move in whichever way we want. The concept of a human robot whose mind and body are obedient to another person's every whim, has become a distinct possibility.

Vocabulary

2 Complete the crossword.

Across

2. She's never afraid to speak her ____.
5. Please don't ____ me when I'm in the middle of telling a joke.
6. The news was so shocking, I was at a ____ for words.
7. I admit, I ____ loudly whenever I see a spider.

Down

1. When I'm tired, I get grumpy and sometimes ____ at people.
2. You should speak more clearly. Don't ____.
3. Please ____; I don't want anyone else to hear us.
4. I can't keep a secret; I ____ things out at the worst times!

Grammar

3a Match the beginning of each sentence with its end to make conditional sentences.

____ 1. If we hadn't missed the plane,
____ 2. If you don't like Coldplay,
____ 3. If you pay for the tickets,
____ 4. If I had plenty of money,
____ 5. If we'd gone to the concert,
____ 6. Unless you pay,
____ 7. If we hadn't managed to get tickets,

a. I'd take a six-month vacation.
b. we wouldn't have seen Coldplay.
c. we would be on vacation now.
d. I'll go to the concert with you.
e. you shouldn't have bought tickets for their show.
f. we would have seen the band.
g. I won't go to the concert with you.

b Answer these questions about the completed sentences in Exercise 3a.

1. Is sentence 1 past unreal conditional or mixed conditional?
2. Is sentence 5 past unreal conditional or mixed conditional?
3. Which type of conditional is sentence 4?
4. Which type of conditional is sentence 2?

4 Complete the second sentence so that it means the same as the first.

Ex: You can put on the life jacket, but only if there is an emergency.

   Don't put on the life jacket _unless there is an emergency._

1. We went to the store sale and bought an incredibly cheap sofa.
   If we hadn't gone _____ .

2. If the neighbors complain, you can't have a party.
   You can have a party _____ .

3. Plants grow when you give them water.
   If you _____ .

4. One day I might get a pay raise, and then I'll be able to buy a nice house.
   If I got a pay raise _____ .

5. We will give you a guarantee if you pay by credit card.
   If _____ .

6. Miguel forgot to turn on his alarm clock so he overslept.
   Miguel wouldn't have overslept _____ _____ .

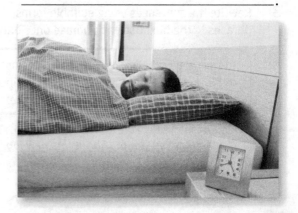

UNIT 10
Review

1 Circle the correct choice.

1. Harold was knocked *subconscious/ unconscious* by the falling tree.

2. Although I had never been there before, I had a strong feeling of *sixth sense/déjà vu*.

3. I always *trust/believe* my intuition about new people I meet.

4. Before we left for the airport, I had an awful *premonition/intuition* that something bad was about to happen.

5. It isn't really difficult to learn new skills; it's just a question of *brain/mind* over matter.

6. You need a lot of *premonition/willpower* to give up smoking.

7. My brother gets very stressed about his work; I think he has a/an *subconscious/unconscious* fear of failure.

8. Hypnotists are experts at using the power of *persuasion/intuition*.

2 Some of the sentences contain mistakes with pronouns. Find and correct the mistakes.

1. Emma cut her while doing the dishes.

2. Mike takes his laptop with himself when he goes on business trips.

3. Juanita and Mario phone each others every day.

4. I'm going to teach myself to play the violin.

5. To save money we painted our house ourself.

6. Mr. and Mrs. Wright decided to take their grandchildren with themselves when they went to the mountains.

7. I have no objections to the product itself; it's the advertisement that annoys me.

8. I repaired me the broken chair.

3 Rewrite the sentences using suitable forms of the phrases in the box. Use each phrase once only.

> to have always believed that   to be against
> to be skeptical about   to be convinced
> ~~to have your doubts about~~   to be in favor of

Ex: Janet isn't really sure about this new job.
Janet has her doubts about this new job.

1. I am absolutely certain that Jimmy is guilty of the crime.

_____

2. Emily supports the idea of longer prison sentences for criminals.

_____

3. All my life I have had the opinion that people are basically honest.

_____

4. Some politicians don't support the new tax.

_____

5. I really don't completely trust or believe in hypnosis.

_____

4 Complete the crossword.

Across

2. I found a used car for a good price in the _____ section of the paper.

5. For this product, our target _____ is teenagers.

7. She works in _____. She determines where and how to sell her company's products.

Down

1. The company spends $2 million a year on _____ in magazines and on TV.

2. A _____ is an advertisement shown between TV shows.

3. A _____ is a short clever phrase used by advertisers or politicians.

4. _____ is publicity that makes something seem more important than it really is.

6. Which _____ is it? Sony or Samsung?

5 Complete the sentences with the correct forms of the words in parentheses.

1. Jane's father agreed _____ home from the nightclub. (drive/us)
2. Did you remember _____ before you left? (turn on/the burglar alarm)
3. Have you considered _____ in other countries? (apply/to universities)
4. We regret _____ that your job application has been unsuccessful. (inform/you)
5. My grandfather continued _____ until he was 80. (work/as a doctor)
6. It was an expensive city but we enjoyed _____. (live/there)
7. I would avoid _____—they taste disgusting. (eat/the prawns)
8. It was a very long drive, so at one o'clock I stopped _____. (have/lunch)
9. Her new job involves _____ and publicity materials. (design/websites)
10. My teacher persuaded _____ the first certificate exam next summer. (me/take)

6 Match the verbs with their definitions. Two phrases have no definitions.

_____ 1. be at a loss for words
_____ 2. shriek
_____ 3. interrupt
_____ 4. whisper
_____ 5. have a word with
_____ 6. mumble
_____ 7. blurt out
_____ 8. speak your mind

a. to speak quietly because you only want one person to hear you
b. to not know what to say
c. to tell people exactly what you think about something, even if it is shocking
d. to say something quickly without thinking about it
e. to speak quietly and not very clearly
f. to say something while another person is still speaking

7 Circle the correct words to complete the sentences.

1. I'll go to the party ____ you agree to come with me.
   a. unless   c. if not
   b. if
2. If we ____ stuck in this traffic jam, we would be there by now.
   a. didn't get   c. hadn't gotten
   b. don't get
3. If the movie hadn't ended so late, we ____ the last bus home.
   a. would miss   c. don't miss
   b. wouldn't have missed
4. We'll give you a refund ____ back the receipt.
   a. if you bring   c. unless you bring
   b. if you brought
5. If she isn't at home, ____ the invitation through the mailbox.
   a. you would put   c. you have put
   b. put
6. If I ____ to a part-time job, I'd have a lot more time with the children.
   a. changed   c. had changed
   b. will change
7. If you've lived there all your life, you ____ how beautiful it is.
   a. already know   c. already knew
   b. had already known
8. If we'd arrived earlier, we ____ the movie stars arriving.
   a. might see   c. might have seen
   b. saw
9. You shouldn't use that expensive cell phone ____ it's a real emergency.
   a. if
   b. although
   c. unless
10. Darren ____ on the winning team if he hadn't broken his leg.
   a. wasn't
   b. could have been
   c. can be

English in Common 5
Extra Listening Audioscript

The Extra Listening Audio MP3 files and printable Activity Worksheets are provided in both the Student book *ActiveBook* disc and in the Teacher's Resource Book *ActiveTeach* disc. The audio can be accessed by clicking the Extra Listening footer button. The audio files are also available at the end of the Audio Program CDs. The audioscripts are also available as printable files on *ActiveBook* or *ActiveTeach*.

UNIT 1

 2.25

A: Excuse me. Can you help me get this up? I can't manage—it's too heavy for me.

B: Sure, no problem.

A: Thanks. I'm Karen.

B: Jim.

A:/B: Hi. / Nice to meet you.

B: Um, would you prefer the window seat? I'd be happy to change.

A: Thanks, but no thanks! I'm really nervous about flying, so I'd rather not look out!

B: You must not be a frequent flyer, then.

A: Actually, I'm a financial consultant, and I fly all the time for work—can't drive across the ocean! But this is personal travel—my brother is working in Seoul, and I've never been to Korea, so I'm grabbing a few days before going on to Japan for work. You know, it's funny—no one in my family likes to fly, but somehow all of us ended up living in different parts of the world. Thank goodness for e-mail and cell phones!

B: And how! Where does the rest of your family live?

A: I have a really big family. How much time do you have?

B: Well, we have 15 hours till Seoul . . .

A: OK, then. Well, where should I start? My parents divorced when I was a child, and are both remarried . . .

B: Wow, you really do have a far-flung family! Your mother and step-dad are in Hawaii, working for the US Navy. Your half-sister's a successful actress in Hollywood . . .

A: . . . but she's making a movie in Canada now. And my step-brother is a foreign correspondent for CNN. He's always on the move.

B: Must be an exciting job.

A: Uh-huh, it's definitely exciting, but it's not for everyone. It can be dangerous and at times pretty lonely. He's away from his partner for weeks at a time. And what about you? Where do you live?

B: Me? Right here in New York, the Big Apple! I moved here right after college, and worked part time while I got my MBA.

A: Where did you grow up?

B: In the Midwest, on a farm. All of my family is still there.

A: You must miss them.

B: Yeah, I do, but we stay in touch, and I visit them a couple of times a year. The thing is, we don't exactly see eye to eye politically, so it's better to have a little distance between us.

A: Yeah, I know what you mean.

B: It sounds like somebody is sleeping. What time is it? Oh wow—we've been talking for five hours. I had no idea!

A: *Five hours?* Sorry, I don't mean to be rude, but I'd like to catch up on some sleep. Do you mind?

B: Not a problem. I could use some shut eye myself. See you in Seoul.

UNIT 2

▶ 2.26

A: Good morning, listeners. I'm Sue Lee and this is "Our Times."

Today I'll be talking to two people who lost their jobs in the economic downturn but saw an opportunity to follow their dreams. Our first guest, Laura Richards, was a highly-paid financial analyst. Now she makes jewelry and sells her pieces on-line. Laura, it's been two years since you became an entrepreneur and started your own business. Can you tell us about your experience?

B: Hi, Sue. Well, I must say that it's been a lot tougher than I expected. I made jewelry as a hobby on the weekends as a way to relax and be creative. Nowadays, in addition to making necklaces, bracelets, and earrings, I'm busy with financial planning and accounting, updating my web site, and mailing packages. I do a lot of the same stuff that I used to, but now it's all for my own business, not someone else's. It's exhausting, but I love it. I'm going to be starting home-sale parties soon, but I'll have to hire a marketing manager for that. I don't have time to do anything but work. I have no free time at all!

A: Wow! Sounds like starting a small business can be grueling! And you really have to be a self-starter. So tell me, if you had the chance, would you go back to banking?

B: No way! This work is much more creative and challenging. I may fail, but at least I can't be laid off again!

A: Our second guest, Matt Young, had a job on Wall Street as a stockbroker. After he was laid off, he became a personal trainer. You look like you're in great shape, Matt! You must get a lot of exercise and eight hours of sleep a night, right? And no stress—not like the old days on Wall Street.

C: Well, Sue thanks for the compliment. But your comment about getting more sleep, unfortunately, isn't the case. When I was a broker, I used to be on the trading floor by seven AM, looking at the Asian and European markets, but in those days, my day ended at five. Now my days are longer. I start at six AM. In fact, many of my clients are former co-workers, and I don't often finish until eight PM on some days.

A: Those are long hours!

C: Yeah.

A: So why do it?

C: Well, I guess I like what I'm doing, and I feel I'm making a difference now; that people are healthier because of me. And I can see actual results which I couldn't as a broker. I try to bring out the best in my clients. I help them to eat right, you know, cutting back on fried food and sweets like French fries and ice-cream, and I get them to exercise at least three times a week. I push them to do the best that they can!

A: So you won't go back to the Market for the big bucks any time soon?

C: No, that is unless paying the rent becomes a problem and I have to.

UNIT 3

 2.26

A: Hi, everyone. This is Joy Briggs. Today we're talking with Chef David Young, the author of *Cooking around the World*. David, I see that you've included some tidbits of food history and folklore in your new book, along with the recipes—makes your book very lively reading, even for someone like me who doesn't like to cook!

B: Yes, I love finding out where common ingredients come from. You may think you know about them, but often you don't.

A: Can you give me an example?

B: Take spaghetti, for instance.

A: Oh, that one's easy. It's not Italy. Marco Polo brought pasta back with him from his travels in China, right?

B: Well, you know, that's actually a myth. Marco Polo may have made pasta popular, but food historians now think that the first pasta was brought to Italy by Arabs invading Sicily in the 8th century. The ancestor of spaghetti was a kind of dried noodle similar to ramen.

A: Really?! That's a surprise. Well, then, is it true that some of our most common everyday foods actually come from Peru?

B: Yes, it is. When the Spanish explorers, or conquistadors, went to South America, they were looking for gold, but they actually found something much more valuable—potatoes and tomatoes. Believe it or not, these were unknown in Europe before 1536.

A: How about that! I can't imagine Spanish food without potatoes and tomatoes. They're basic ingredients.

B: I know. And to think that the potato is the fourth largest food crop in the world. And back in 1995, the potato became the first vegetable to be grown in space. Future space travelers will be able to snack on potato chips!

A: And what about . . .

UNIT 4

▶ **2.28**

A: Man, these kids are a lively bunch. Still full of energy and it was an eight-hour bus trip! I don't think I had that much energy in high school. They make me feel ancient and I'm only 24! OK, here comes our group, Jon. Good luck!

B: Hi, everyone! I'm Jon, and this is Sue. We're your Outward Bound leaders for the next week. We're going to start by explaining some of our rules, and then answer all of your questions. Ready?

Voices: Yeah. Sure. OK.

B: All right. First, we're going to be doing lots of challenging, and sometimes dangerous, sports and activities. You'll be going backcountry hiking, whitewater rafting, kayaking, and rock climbing— things a lot of you city kids have probably never done. All of these activities have the potential for serious accidents. This means you have to think about what you're doing at all times, understood?

A: So rule number 1 is safety first. Guys, please listen to instructions carefully, and if Jon or I say "Stop," stop first, and ask questions later! Understood?

Voices: Yep. /Uh-huh/ Got it.

B: And Rule 2 is all equipment must be checked and rechecked daily.

C: Why do we have to do that?

A: Simple! We don't want anyone falling off a mountain because of a broken rope! OK?

Voices: Yes, yeah, sure, understood.

B: Rule 3: we have a buddy system here. You work with a buddy. You shouldn't go anywhere alone. Your buddy is responsible for you, and you're responsible for him. Never go near water, into the woods, up a hill—anywhere alone. We'll talk more about this later.

A: And Rule 4 is that we always respect the environment. We're a green organization.

D: Can you explain that?

A: Sure. It means we clean up after ourselves, and we don't leave garbage behind. Whatever you take into the wilderness, you bring back out, including plastic wraps and bottle caps. In fact, we refill and reuse all our water bottles. And we use soaps and cleaning products that are biodegradable, and that don't contaminate the land or water. We're visitors to this beautiful land, and we want to leave it beautiful for the people who follow us. Got it?

D: Yeah. Thanks.

B: OK. Just a few more things before we get started . . .

UNIT 5

▶ 2.29

A: Hi, Eileen. Is something the matter? You're looking kind of upset.

B: Hi, Dan, I'm not really upset; I'm just disappointed. I just spent two hours uploading over 150 vacation and family photos to my computer, and most of them are pretty bad.

A: Do you want me to take a look at some of them? I'll be happy to give you some tips.

B: Would you? That would be wonderful! Thanks. Here's one of my sister and her birthday cake. Boy, is her face red!

A: Well, that's no surprise—twenty candles are a lot to blow out! But, what else do you notice about the picture?

B: Well, um, a lot of people at the table have their eyes closed, and they look so serious, even though I did I ask them to say "cheese!"

A: Well, you've got a choice. You can take a candid shot, and get this result. Or you can do what I do.

B: What's that?

A: Tell everyone to close their eyes and to open them at the count of three. If you do it that way, they'll all be smiling, and you'll get a great picture.

B: Good idea! I'll definitely try that next time. Oh, now look at these ones at the beach. The children were having so much fun jumping in the waves, but all the pictures are blurry.

A: Again, that's no surprise. Kids move! If you want to get the movement, then take a video next time.

B: Oh, of course. My phone can do that.

A: And Eileen?

B: What?

A: Here's the biggest secret: you don't have to keep every picture you take. Delete the bad ones right away. And only share the best ones with your friends.

B: Is that what you do?

A: Uh-huh. That's my secret. I keep enough to make a small album and get rid of the rest.

B: So how many of my 150 will I end up with?

A: Maybe 30 or so.

B: That's all?

UNIT 6

▶ 2.30

A: Good morning, listeners. Steve Ross here on *Talking Business*, Radio WAMB. Today our special guest is Gary Hunter, president and CEO of *Work Abroad*. His firm helps find jobs around the world for college students who recently graduated or are taking a year off from school. Welcome, Gary!

B: Hi, Steve. Good to be here.

A: Gary, can you give our listeners some tips on what to do if they'd like to move overseas?

B: Sure, Steve. Well, I guess the first and most important thing to think about is why you want to work abroad. What's your motivation? Are you interested in a particular country? Do you speak the language or want to learn it? Do you want to advance your career or mostly have fun?

A: Good questions!

B: Second, I tell them to remember three very important words.

A: And they are . . . ?

B: Network, network, and network! Usually, *what* you know isn't as important as *who* you know. You need connections. Think about your network of friends, or friends of friends who live or have lived where you want to go. Maybe you have distant family you can call on who might help you find work—or your parents' co-workers may have business contacts you can talk to.

A: Okaaaay. . . . Now the phones are open to hear some stories from our listeners. . . . Hello, Alicia from Miami. Success or failure?

C: Success! I found a job teaching acting in Hanoi.

A: How'd you do that?

C: Well, I went to Vietnam on a summer exchange program, and a group of us decided to put on a play for fellow students.

A: In English?

C: Oh, yes, of course. I don't speak much Vietnamese.

A local theater director who runs an English language school saw me act, and the rest is history. Now I direct, act and teach—my students put on one-act plays in English.

A: Thanks for the call, Alicia. Gary, is that an unusual way to find a job?

B: Actually, it's not uncommon. A lot of young people go overseas through a volunteer or low-paid position with a non-profit organization, like Alicia did, and then make contact with a local company or school. Of course, most of these backpacker Americans, Australians, Canadians, and Brits end up teaching English.

A: Our next caller wasn't so lucky. Go ahead Jane.

D: Well, I was an *au pair* in Paris. The children were horrible! I couldn't believe . . .

UNIT 7

 2.31

1. **A:** Jones' Sporting Goods. May I help you?

   B: I certainly hope so! I'm calling about a defective football. I kicked it and whoosh!

   A: I'm sorry. What do you mean "whoosh"?

   B: All the air came out; it went completely flat!

   A: I've never heard of a ball doing that. Did your shoe have a sharp nail in it?

   B: Absolutely not! The ball was defective.

   A: I'm terribly sorry, sir. Just bring it back to the store and we'll give you a new one.

2. **C:** I can't believe I wasted a whole beautiful sunny day.

   D: What were you doing?

   C: Odds and ends—housework, laundry, some food shopping, and waiting for a plumber to fix a leaky faucet—just stupid stuff I don't have time for during the week.

   D: Poor thing! Well, I had a great day. I played tennis in the morning and then met friends for lunch. Maybe you can get out tomorrow.

   C: Yeah, right. The weather report says it's going to rain all day.

3. **E:** Hello, Half Price Hotels, Jim speaking.

   F: Hello, Jim. I'm calling because I just tried to book a hotel in London online for two weeks from now. I filled in all the information, and then the site froze up. This has happened twice. It's really frustrating!

   E: I'm so sorry. We'll have a technician check it out. In the meantime, why don't you give me your name and credit card information, and I'll process the reservation.

   F: Thanks. It's a Visa card, number 4359 . . .

UNIT 8

▶ 2.32

A: Good evening, class. Tonight as part of our study of family relationships, we'll look at different ways of raising children. I asked you to read several articles comparing Asian and Western parenting styles. Who would like to start the discussion?

B: I'll start. I read Amy Chua's article, "Why Chinese Moms are Superior." She thinks Chinese, and other Asian mothers, raise more successful, disciplined children. She calls these mothers "Tiger Moms" and followed their lead in bringing up her two daughters.

A: Can you summarize what she said?

B: Yes, I think so. Her main point was that Asian parents are generally stricter than Western parents. They really stress educational excellence. They insist that their children get As in school. This means that their kids spend so much time studying that they don't have time for extracurricular activities, like sports or being in a school play

A: Thank you. Would someone else continue?

C: I will. Professor Chua said that her children had to learn to play the piano or the violin—no other instrument. And they had to practice two or three hours a day.

D: And they couldn't watch TV or play computer games.

A: Sounds like a tough approach, doesn't it? In fact, her essay is meant to be humorous, but a lot of readers took it very seriously, and there were some pretty strong reactions. So what do you think about her ideas? Do you agree with her? What about you, Susan?

D: Well, at first I thought it was awful! I think that most American parents think it's important for their children to be well-rounded. You know, that academics aren't everything. After all, physical and social development are equally important. And to do this means kids have to be involved in lots of after school activities, like being on a football or swim team, or singing in a choir. And, best of all, sleepovers with friends on the weekends. I loved those when I was young.

A: But . . . ?

D: But, to be honest, my study skills weren't too great. I had a lot of trouble in school. I spent more time hanging out at the mall than in the library. That's why I'm back in this class at the age of 30!

C: Yeah, me too. I was so busy with soccer practice during the week and games on the weekend, that I hardly had time for schoolwork. It can't be all work or all play—I mean, there's got to be a happy medium.

UNIT 9

 2.33

1. **A:** What's that?

   B: It's my journal from our trip we took to Europe when we were 19.

   A: It's hard to believe that that was 10 years ago. We were so young!

   B: And so foolish! Do you remember the time we hitched a ride from Paris to Marseille?

   A: And it turned out that the driver had stolen the car, and we provided cover for him?

   B: Yeah, the police were looking for a single man, not three people.

   A: We were really lucky that nothing bad happened. He dropped us off on the outskirts of town and disappeared. In fact, I thought he was a really nice guy—and cute, too. I'd have given him my phone number if he'd asked for it.

   B: I wonder what ever happened to him. Do you think he was caught eventually?

2. **A:** I just heard that we're going to be hit by a hurricane on Wednesday or Thursday. Everyone in our neighborhood has to evacuate again.

   B: Uh-uh. Not me. This time I'm not leaving. I'm afraid that looters might take advantage of my empty house. Remember what happened to my brother-in-law a few years ago? He came home to find his TV and computers were stolen. They even took his steaks in his freezer! And then they left the freezer door open, so everything else spoiled. It was a real mess.

   A: Well, if you stay, you might get in trouble with the law. The mayor issued an order that everyone had to go to higher ground. In any case, you're insured, aren't you? You can replace things, it's only money, but you can't replace your life. Think about what could happen: there might be flooding, a power line or tree could fall on you.

   B: I guess you're right. Better safe than sorry!

3. **A:** Did I tell you that my friend, Rose, was conned last week.

   B: Conned? Really? Did she lose a lot of money?

   A: No, not really. Actually, it's really a funny story. A middle-aged, kind of seedy-looking man stopped her on the street and said he wanted to make a five-dollar bet with her. He said he knew where she got her shoes.

   B: What did she do? Did she take the bet?

   A: Well, Rose had bought her shoes in Italy, so she said, "OK, guess where I got them."

   B: And? Did she win the bet?

   A: Listen to this: the man said, "You got your shoes on the sidewalk, right here! That'll be five dollars, please."

   B: Did your friend pay up?

   A: Yep. She said it was worth the money. Now she's enjoying telling everyone that a word trick cost her five dollars.

   B: So . . . I bet I can tell you where you got . . .

UNIT 10

▶ 2.34

A: Good morning friends. Our topic today is the extraordinary perception of animals. Believe it or not, there does seem to be some hard evidence that animals can sense when an earthquake is about to happen. As far back as 373 BC, the Greeks noted unusual animal behavior prior to a significant earthquake. Please welcome someone with more recent experience, our guest, David Nelson. David is an animal keeper at the national zoo in Washington D.C.

B: Thank you.

A: David, did the animals react to the magnitude 5.8 earthquake that hit the capital in 2011?

B: Yes, every animal, except for the giant pandas, sensed that something was wrong. Most, like the lions, snakes, and elephants, acted strangely as soon as the quake started, but some seemed to know it was coming while everything still seemed normal. For example, I was just starting to feed the great apes—and they love to eat—when Kyle, an orangutan, and Kojo, a gorilla, abandoned their food and climbed to the top of the tree in their area. That was five to ten seconds before the quake started. And three seconds before the shaking began, Mandara, a gorilla, let out a loud shriek, picked up her baby, Kibibi, and climbed the tree, too.

A: I guess they feel safer at the top of a tree than on the ground! What about other animals?

B: This one is really strange. The red ruffled lemurs sounded an alarm call about 15 minutes before the quake started, and then again just as it happened. And our 64 flamingos rushed into a group and huddled together seconds before the quake started. They stayed close together until the shaking stopped.

A: So it seems clear that some animals, at least, can sense a change in the air or ground before an earthquake is about to start. Do you think we can find a way to use this ability to predict when the next one will hit?